Enfant Terrible
THE LIFE AND WORLD OF
Maurice Utrillo

Nonfiction Books by
Peter de Polnay

BY PETER DE POLNAY

Enfant Terrible
THE LIFE AND WORLD OF
Maurice Utrillo

WILLIAM MORROW AND COMPANY, INC.
NEW YORK
1969

—— To Robert Naly

Preface

SHORTLY after Suzanne Valadon's death in 1938 Robert Naly, as an intimate friend of her remarkable family, was asked to write a book on Valadon, André Utter her husband and Maurice Utrillo her son. Naly refused, saying that he was a painter, not a writer. When I told him that I intended to write *Enfant Terrible* he put all his material and the resources of his excellent memory at my disposal. Without him and the admirable help of my wife Carmen this book could not have been born.

I knew Utrillo and his wife Lucie Valore, was well acquainted with his stepfather André Utter and lived for years in their world on the Butte-Montmartre and among their close friends. The air he had breathed for most of his life was the air that filled my lungs too. And while on the Butte, I accepted its tenets and values, however false or exaggerated they may have seemed from outside.

Among Utrillo's biographers, Adolphe Tabarant, Francis Carco and Gustave Coquiot are outstanding, but not one of them went beyond the year 1928. Tabarant came nearest to the painter, Carco to the legend and Coquiot to the man.

This book contains nothing I have not seen, heard, read or been told. I had to swim carefully in a sea of contradictions, lies and calumny. Many people appeared to have an axe to grind. I discovered that there was a Valadon Party, an Utter Party and a Valore Party. The only one who had no party was Utrillo himself. He was too busy painting.

I am deeply grateful to Messieurs Jean Abegg, Lars Bo, William de Cazenave, Henri-Georges Cheval, Paul Gérard, Robert and Pierre Giraud, Henri Leduc, André Malterre, Jean Pompougnac, Jean Vertex and Gilbert Gruet of the Galerie Bernheim-Jeune, who have all been of true help to me while I was writing this book.

In spite of his advanced age Michel Georges-Michel, the author of *De Renoir à Picasso, les peintres que j'ai connu, Chefs-d'oeuvre de Peintres Contemporains,* et cetera, received me with great kindness and recalled the days when he and Utrillo were young men and painted together. Mme. Andrée Metthey, widow of my late friend Jean Metthey, was immensely helpful. If they were still alive I would also offer my thanks to Pedro Creixams, Jean Dufy and, of course, André Utter.

I have to acknowledge my debt to the excellent staff of the Salle de Travail and the Cabinet des Estampes of the Bibliothèque Nationale of Paris.

Utrillo's was an extraordinary life. "I cannot believe that Utrillo exists," a friend of Tabarant observed, after Tabarant had described some of Utrillo's escapades.

"His paintings prove that he does," Tabarant replied.

Contents

Illustrations

The illustrations appear between pages 64 and 65.

Enfant Terrible
THE LIFE AND WORLD OF
Maurice Utrillo

The Terrible Maria

1

MADELEINE-CÉLINA VALADON, Suzanne Valadon's
mother and Maurice Utrillo's grandmother, was born
on December 9, 1830, in Bessines-sur-Gartempe, a small market
town in the *arrondissement* of Bellac in the department of
Haute-Vienne. The town was surrounded by fields and farms
and populated by cautious peasants who took nothing for
granted; their favorite proverb was, "A dog barks when it is
afraid."

Madeleine was of humble stock and entered domestic service
when still in her teens. She married a man named Coulon who
was arrested around 1851 for a felony he had committed, sen-
tenced to life imprisonment and died while serving his sentence.
Madeleine reverted to her maiden name and was thirty-five
when her daughter Marie-Clémentine was born on September
23, 1865. Marie-Clémentine Valadon was Suzanne Valadon's
real Christian name. She was baptized the day after her birth.
The birth certificate records, "Father unknown."

Madeleine was employed as a washerwoman in the bourgeois household of a Monsieur Duclos and his family. She excelled in ironing and starching shirts. In the year 1869 she decided to leave Bessines for good and brave the capital with her small daughter.

The "haussmannization" of Paris was in full swing and many Limousins worked in the capital as masons and bricklayers. Aided and abetted by the Emperor Napoleon III, Baron Georges Haussmann, for seventeen years Prefect of the Seine Department, transformed old districts and added new ones. Those who loathed seeing their old walls, streets and gardens go called it "haussmannization." The process continued after Haussmann left; in fact it still goes on. Parisians can say ruefully, "The baron is always with us," but he was a godsend for the poor who flocked to Paris in search of work.

It seems quite extraordinary for a peasant woman, with a small child to support, to uproot herself and leave her native Limousin for the metropolis. However, as Suzanne Valadon would come to relate, there was a friend of her mother's, also a Limousin, who worked on a construction site in Paris. Madeleine found someone to write to him, for she could neither read nor write. The foreman replied, suggesting she come to Paris and start a laundry. The reason Valadon gave for her mother leaving the Duclos household was that Monsieur Duclos had lost all his money in the Panama Scandal and could no longer afford servants. However, there was no truth in it, since Ferdinand de Lesseps did not embark on the Panama venture until 1881, twelve years after Madeleine and her daughter had left Bessines.

Here we begin to encounter the lies and mystifications with which Valadon surrounded herself from childhood onward. She was not a liar in the strict sense of the word, but a romancer and a storyteller who believed her own stories. She maintained that her mother brought her to Paris in a pannier. But she was already four years old when Madeleine set out for Paris, too big to be

carried in a pannier. Still, a pannier sounds more romantic than
a hard third-class railway bench and it fitted in with another
story of hers: till her dying day she swore that she was born
in 1867 and not in 1865. A two-year-old could still have travelled in a pannier.

The illegitimate child has one advantage—he can invent his
father. Valadon went one better: now and then, if she was in
her storytelling mood, she *un*invented her mother. She told her
listeners that she had been a foundling, discovered in a basket
on the steps of Limoges Cathedral, and entrusted to various
wet nurses till she ended up with a decent woman named Madeleine-Célina Valadon whom she called Grandmother. Nobody
knew, she said, who her real mother was. Burnt by the sun of
summer and lashed by the icy winter winds of Limousin, Madeleine had aged quickly. At thirty-nine a peasant woman looked
old in those days. It was easy for Valadon with her imagination
to look on Madeleine as her grandmother. Apart from the story
of the basket on the steps of Limoges Cathedral, Valadon brought
no memories from her native Limousin. Her life, as it were,
began in Paris.

More surprising and astonishing than any tale Valadon invented was the very fact that Madeleine, who had never left
Bessines before, now departed for good. Maybe the Limousin
foreman did exist, but was his presence in the capital enough
to give her the strength to take the plunge? She was nearly
forty when she set out on the road to a new life. Whatever
force drew her to Paris, it must have been powerful enough to
overcome the peasant's instinctive fear of being uprooted.

Madeleine and her daughter found lodgings near the Bastille,
where they stayed until the Franco-Prussian War. The poor
leave no marks; it is not recorded exactly where they lodged.
Before the Commune they moved to Montmartre, some say to
the rue du Poteau, others to the rue de Clignancourt. The two
streets are not far apart. Coming from the rue du Poteau one
had only to cross the square, go past the newly built church of

Notre-Dame-de-Clignancourt, a church Utrillo would come to love deeply, and walk a couple of hundred yards down the rue Ordoner to reach the rue de Clignancourt. They had also lived in the Boulevard de Rochechouart for a while. Madeleine set herself up as a laundress, and because she ironed and starched exceptionally well she soon had a large clientele.

Paris was not yet overpopulated; there were many other districts they could have settled in. They possessed nothing, were unencumbered by the considerations, preferences or idiosyncrasies that make one select a particular neighbourhood. They had no special needs, except for Madeleine to earn a living for the two of them. Yet Montmartre became their home.

2

"Montmartre," the Montmartrois say, "has a very special spirit of its own."

When Madeleine and her little daughter reached Montmartre a fresh wind was blowing on the hillock, due once again to the Baron Haussmann. Montmartre, which was separated from Paris by the Wall of the Fermiers-Généraux, had remained a village throughout the centuries. However, in 1860 the Baron persuaded the Emperor Napoleon III to attach to Paris the outlying parishes of Batignolles, Monceaux, Montmartre, Belleville, Ménilmontant, Neuilly, Les Gobelins and Montrouge. The Walls were pulled down. They had divided the parish of Montmartre into two districts: Montmartre *intra muros* (Low Montmartre) and Montmartre *extra muros* (High Montmartre). The population of High Montmartre was rustic and friendly, consisting of millers, vinegrowers, labourers and quarry men; the inhabitants of Low Montmartre were a turbulent crowd of tavern and cabaret keepers, ruffians and frequenters of dance halls and *guinguettes*. *Guinguettes* were taverns with gardens, where one danced and drank; they were named after one Guinguet, who had such an establishment at Ménilmontant around 1640. With the Walls gone, access to the Butte—that is, High Montmartre —became easier and quicker for the Low Montmartrois. Whereas the rustics had little inclination to come down, the blackguards and the harlots left the cabarets and made for the hillock. They were followed, quite independently, by the *lorettes*.

The name *lorette* was given to the kept women of Low Montmartre because most of them hailed from the Notre-Dame-de-Lorette neighbourhood. They were noisy, vulgar women whose antics flushed some of the *bourgeoisie* out of Montmartre. Les Porcherons, as the district extending between the rue du Faubourg Montmartre and Saint-Lazare was known as before the Walls came down, had been their spiritual home. "It is Monday; yesterday in the Porcherons the man drank a wine full of fury, shouts and curses," wrote Victor Hugo of the home of the *lorettes*.

In the new Paris without walls it fell to the Butte to receive these girls. They must have looked out of their windows one bright morning and exclaimed: "Lo! The Walls are down." Then, lifting their skirts, they skipped up the slope.

In her childhood and early youth Valadon breathed the same air as the *lorettes*. She saw them in the cobbled, twisting streets and in her mother's laundry when they brought their linen— and their lovers' linen—to be washed. She was too much the born artist to be unaffected by their flamboyant, picturesque essence and presence. She saw them leaning out of the windows of the new houses of the neighbourhood. Proprietors of fresh buildings allowed the *lorettes* to live in them till plaster and paint had dried and the apartments were ready to be let to more respectable tenants.

The *lorettes* installed themselves, giving Montmartre a scandalous, new reputation. The story goes that an old beggarwoman of Montmartre remarked to a gentleman when thanking him for his charity, "God guard your son, sir, from our daughters."

The *lorettes* were described as neither wives nor spinsters, but, strictly speaking, they were not prostitutes. They were daughters of tradesmen and artisans who escaped to a freer life on the mountain, most of them taking up with artists and bohemians who had also invaded Montmartre. They lived with their men, deserted them for others or were deserted in their turn, and when the holiday was over they either went back to their families, provided their families were willing to receive them, or drifted into wretchedness, which would normally leave them in the hospital or in the Seine. But while it lasted, theirs was a flamboyant life, a constant challenge to middle-class virtues. Gavarni immortalized them in his drawings and paintings, Balzac in *Grandeurs et misères des courtisanes*.

In the new Montmartre where Madeleine settled with her four-year-old daughter, there was little left of the old. The Mons Martis of the Romans, called after the temple of Mars they had built next to their temple of Mercury, and the Mons Martyrum named after the martyrdom of St. Denis, St. Eleuthère and St. Rustique, were now no more than material for discussions among etymologists. The bombardment of Paris by Henri IV from the top of Montmartre was history, and the quarries which had honeycombed the mountain—425 feet above sea level at its highest point—were closed when the village was absorbed into Paris and the ground had to be consolidated before haussmannization could attack it. But there still were deep holes in the Maquis, the waste land that stretched from the rue de Caulaincourt to the rue Lepic, and when children went to play there, their parents warned them sternly that if they fell into these holes they would roam forever in dark tunnels and probably meet Marat's ghost. Marat had hidden in the quarries for a fortnight or so shortly after he started to publish *L'Ami du peuple*.

When Madeleine and her child settled down in the rue du Poteau there were still large road signs warning promenaders against precipices and carters against excessive speed.

PRECIPICES!
CAUTION! USE YOUR BRAKES

Even most of the windmills that had covered the slopes and the summit of the Butte for centuries had vanished. Only a few remained, one of them, the Moulin de la Galette which had been built in 1275 and had originally been called Blute-Fin. When in 1814 the Allies marched on Paris, Russian troops assaulted the Moulin de la Galette. It was defended by the Debray family, who claimed to have been millers there from the time it was built. They stood their ground heroically when the Cossacks attacked. Though the eldest son was killed and his corpse hanged from a sail, the rest of the family and other defenders of the mill succeeded in reaching Marshall Moncey and his dragoons at the Barrière de Clichy. The defense of the Moulin de la Galette became one of the highlights of the legend of Montmartre.

"You speak as though you had fought the Cossacks in the Moulin de la Galette," Valadon is reputed to have said to someone who was given to boasting.

After the Napoleonic wars the Debray family returned to the Moulin, though they no longer milled grain. They found it easier to sell milk and girdle-cakes (*galettes*) to the strollers and promenaders, especially to young lovers who came up the Butte. That was the first step. The second was to provide the customers with wine, and when it rained the good folk were allowed to take shelter inside the mill. It soon had many patrons.

There had been taverns and *guinguettes* on the Butte as early as the seventeenth century. They were frequented by the *mauvais garçons*—the bad boys, rogues, pimps and thieves. For the bad boys of Paris the Butte was a convenient refuge. The Moulin de la Galette might have become just another drinking house if one of the Debrays, known as *"le petit père* Debray," had not been a dedicated enthusiast of dancing. He vowed to transform the mill into a "temple of Terpsichore." He surrounded himself with young people whom he taught the art for the pleasure it gave him. Some time passed before it occurred to him to turn the "temple" into a profitable business. His mill became Le Bal du Moulin de la Galette, a popular dance hall, the inside of which was to be painted by Renoir and the outside many times by Utrillo.

In Montmartre, now the 18th *arrondissement* of Paris, life was free, easy and cheap, and more and more artists, *lorettes* and ruffians flocked to the Butte. Then suddenly in 1870 came the Franco-Prussian War, and not long afterward the Commune and the Siege.

On Saturday, March 18, 1871, the first day of the Commune, rumour spread through Paris that the government troops from Versailles were on the march against the capital. Up on the Butte a few companies of the National Guard guarded the cannons. The people did not want the cannons to fall into hands of the government troops, in fact wanted them to be used in the defense of the Commune. General Lecomte and his staff were taken prisoner as they were suspected of sympathizing with the legal government of the country. The streets were filled with a drunken, armed, excited mob. The National Guardsmen began to fraternize with the people, allowing women and children, especially women, into their ranks. The mob was mad with wine. At four in the afternoon another general wearing civilian clothes, General Thomas, was recognized, arrested and locked up with General Lecomte. Then the furies that excite and lead mobs whipped the crowd forward. Bellowing and shrieking, it surged on, bandits, prostitutes and ponces of the fortifications, a wild raging throng that penetrated into the small house where the generals were under arrest, dragged the two unfortunate men to the rue des Rosiers, now rue du Chevalier de la Barre, put them against a wall and shot them.

"They faced death with a jaunty air," recorded an eyewitness, "heads high, eyes proud, true soldiers." Then the mob caught sight of an officer of *chasseurs* on horseback. They threw themselves on horse and rider, bringing both down, and tore the horse to pieces. The women fought for scraps of meat and the lucky ones rushed straight home to fry their trophies.

One would like to picture Madeleine and her little daughter

in the crowd, Madeleine one of the lucky ones, hurrying home with child and horsemeat, but it seems no such experience ever fired Valadon's imagination, or surely people would have heard of it. Most likely, on that fateful day in March, she was playing down in the rue du Poteau with one of the rag dolls her mother had made her. What is certain is that she was now part of the Montmartre of saints and martyrs, holiness and violence, *lorettes*, blackguards and creative artists.

3

Montmartre was moving toward its golden age and its spirit was frantically beckoning to all who had or thought they had a talent. Hector Berlioz, the composer, had been drawn to the Butte decades before. Alas, his little house at the corner of the rue Saint-Vincent and the rue Saint-Denis, now rue Mont-Cenis, which Utrillo was to paint many times, was pulled down when latter-day haussmannization reached the neighbourhood. Only a tablet on the wall of a vast block of flats indicates that Berlioz loved, quarrelled and composed there. He lived there with Harriet Smithson, the English actress, whom he sighed over for six years, and finally married against the wishes of their families. He and his Harriet kept open house: Chopin, Alfred de Vigny, Liszt and Eugène Sue were among their guests. But love triumphant turned into nagging and stormy scenes, which did not, however, prevent him from composing *Harold in Italy, Benvenuto Cellini, Le Paysan, La Esmeralda* and the *Requiem* for the funeral of General Damremont.

When Berlioz left his English wife he went to live in the rue de Londres. Harriet remained on the Butte, moving to a house lower down in the rue Saint-Vincent. The windows overlooked the old cemetery of Montmartre; when she died in 1854 the old cemetery took her bones.

Gérard de Nerval, the poet, was drawn to the Butte by the

vineyards and the quarries. The wine the Montmartre grapes produced was of inferior quality.

> *C'est du vin de Montmartre*
> *qui en boit pinte en pisse quatre . . .*

went a seventeenth-century jingle. Still it fired Nerval's imagination. "Saint-Denis," he said in a mock funeral oration at the sale of a vineyard, "was from the philosophers' point of view probably the second Bacchus." He described a quarry as a druidic temple. "As the eye becomes accustomed to the depth, one trembles, expecting Esus, Thot or Cérunnes, the redoubtable gods of our ancestors, to emerge." He was fond of the tramps who spent their nights in the quarries. "A thief," he wrote, "always knows where to lay his head. Only honest vagabonds who dared not ask for shelter and drunks who, coming down from the Butte, had no strength to crawl any farther, were arrested in the quarries."

He waxed enthusiastic about the mills, the cabarets, the rustic inns with their gardens, the trees, the fields and the goats. He thought that the natives had the gait of mountaineers, admired the girls with their proud looks, and sighed over the vineyards, which yearly diminished in number. Nowadays there is a tiny vineyard situated in the rue des Saules; enough to provoke a mild nostalgia.

Nerval spent some time in the private lunatic asylum of a Dr. Blanche on the Butte. He was released on the intervention of the Société des Gens de Lettres in the autumn of 1854. It might have been better for French poetry if the society had not intervened. Only a few months later, on January 25 of the following year, he wrote to his aunt: "Do not expect me tonight, for the night will be black and white." Then, instead of finding his way to the grotto where the siren swims, he went to the rue de la Vieille Lanterne and hanged himself from a lamppost.

Montmartre continued to prepare itself for the great dawn.

Down in Low Montmartre, where nobody could boast of the gait of a mountaineer, the painters of the École Indépendante, later to be known as the impressionists, met at the Café Guerbois in the Grand' rue des Batignolles, now the Boulevard de Clichy. This was in the years preceding the Franco-Prussian War. There were two contingents—the first, the old boys of the Académie Suisse, brought there by Frédéric Bazille and Edmond Maître; the second, recruited by Renoir and Claude Monet—both of whom sat at the feet of Édouard Manet and Degas, who had just come back from Italy. Degas visited the café on Fridays; Pissarro made rare appearances, usually accompanied by Cézanne, with whom he often painted in the country.

Manet exhorted the group to paint in "luminous patches" and to "soften the scale of values," revolutionary talk which made the pundits of the old school gasp with indignation and shake with rage. War was declared between the old and the new.

The years of fighting the past and advancing toward the future produced paintings which were akin to manifestos. Théodore Fantin-Latour painted *L'Atelier aux Batignolles* and Manet the portrait of Zacharie Astruc, a mediocre poet, composer and art critic, but champion of the new movement. In Manet's painting we see Otto Schoelderer, Auguste Renoir, Émile Zola, Edmond Maître, Frédéric Bazille and Claude Monet. Remarkably, Fantin-Latour does not appear. Perhaps he was afraid to be identified too closely with the revolutionaries in spite of his early fervour. Moreover, he was doing well by this time. The impressionists were hunted by their enemies; the first victim was Bazille. He was not destroyed by the old guard: he was killed in a skirmish in the Franco-Prussian War, aged only twenty-nine.

The Café Guerbois became too noisy. Marcelin-Gilbert Desboutin, the painter and engraver, described the Boulevard de Clichy as a street of shrieking, drunken crowds. He thought the Guerbois too near to Wepler, Boivin and Père Lathuile, vulgar drinking places, not to mention the Maison Dutrou where cobblers, plumbers and blacksmiths shouted their heads off. It was time to move, and the painters did so in 1870, to La Nouvelle Athènes in the Place Pigalle, where the ceiling had been painted by Petit, a flower painter from the Butte. There at the *apéritif* hour one saw Manet, Degas, Alfred Stevens, young Forain, Félix Buhot, Georges Rivière and Desboutin, with George Moore and Villiers de l'Isle-Adam. Manet painted George Moore seated in the café; Degas painted his absinthe drinkers.

4

Madeleine toiled hard to earn a living. Marseilles soap and the steaming iron kept body and soul together. The life of the poor was difficult, their opportunities few, and in the Paris of Valadon's childhood, starvation was still possible. Another reason to marvel at the illiterate Madeleine's decision to brave the capital.

When André Warnod, who was to become one of the best-known Montmartre writers, arrived with his family at the Gare Saint-Lazare to settle in Paris, he noticed, as they took a fiacre to their new home in Montmartre, a tall cadaverous man whose mien frightened him. His fear grew when he saw the man running behind the carriage. The man followed them to the front door, reaching it simultaneously with the cab. His object was not sinister: he had run the whole way from the station in the hope that he would be allowed to carry the luggage up to the fifth floor and so earn a few sous. He was told he was not needed—the servants would attend to it. He doffed his cap and lolloped back to the station. Perhaps the next train would bring him better luck. That was the world in which Madeleine had to earn the daily bread for herself and her daughter.

Valadon never complained of the poverty that cramped her childhood. She lived humbly and like most children of the poor she spent much time playing in the street, an excellent place for one with observant eyes. If her mother gave her a few centimes she travelled on the *impériale,* the upper deck of the horse-drawn tram, and tore at the leaves of the trees as they brushed past. And there was her drawing.

She was already drawing at the age of eight. She used to spend her Sundays on the roof of the tall block of workers' dwellings where she and Madeleine lived for a while in the Boulevard de Rochechouart, watching the crowds and the merry-go-rounds in the Place d'Anvers. "Like an engraving," she was to say years later. When evening came she went down to their dark, humble abode and drew legs, arms and heads. She was taken to Nantes for a brief period. On her return to Montmartre she was sent to a school run by nuns. Her schooling was not a success: she remained stubbornly uninterested in education. Nothing appealed to her that was not connected with drawing; her sole friend was the coalman because he gave her charcoal. She would go down on her knees in the Place de Ventimille to draw on the pavement the figures she had observed from the roof the previous Sunday. "How did I do that?" she marvelled when reminiscing about her childhood. "Nowadays I couldn't draw even a sugar basin from memory." She did not stay with the nuns for long.

She was a possessive child. Once she threw herself in front of a horse, in order to find out whether Madeleine loved her as fondly as she thought she deserved. The horse shied: Madeleine shrieked: Valadon was delighted. What the coachman thought or said is not recorded.

She was given a sparrow and when it died she wanted to find out whether sparrows were resurrected also. She buried the bird in a garden and visited the grave daily for months, expecting to find the resurrected bird hopping on top of the grave. Eventually she dug it up to see if the ungrateful bird had flown off to Paradise without saying good-by to her.

She was thrown into the hubbub of life straight from school. She believed that she left school at the age of twelve. Her school days meant so little to her that she was not certain when they ended. What she did and how she lived till she became an artist's model is anyone's guess. She told a number of versions of what happened during those intermediate years. One was that she ran away from home; another that she had never slept away from home till she went to live in Montmagny in the nineties. She also said that she had sold vegetables in the Halles, been a waitress in a cheap restaurant, and a nursery maid who took the children of the rich for walks in the Tuileries Gardens. All could be quite true, for twelve was not too young an age to work in those days. Before she was fifteen, she landed in a circus.

A circus was the sort of place that fired her imagination. One day she claimed that she had been an acrobat, the next day she had been a circus rider. None the less, she kept to one story about her reason for leaving the circus: she had fallen off a horse or a trapeze, breaking her leg. The name of the circus varied in every story: in one version it was in Paris, in another, she had joined a travelling circus, fell off the trapeze during a performance in Angoulême and broke her leg. And still another —she had befriended the acrobats of the Cirque Molier in the Place Pigalle who undertook to train her, but she fell off the trapeze in the course of her training. The leg was put in a cast, and while she lay in the hospital, she drew figures on the plaster. The doctor noticed her drawings and, seeing she had great talent, encouraged her. Because of the doctor Valadon began to take her art seriously.

The theater, too, appealed to Valadon and filled her with admiring respect. In her old age she thought that she had been a "rat" at the Opéra in Paris. That was sheer romancing, for the nearest she ever got to the ballet was posing in tutu when she was a model. She could, after all, tell any tale she liked. Laundresses and their children were hampered by neither eye-witnesses nor chroniclers. They went unnoticed, unobserved, no one bothering about their doings. If they suffered poverty they also enjoyed the blessings of liberty, and there is no true liberty without anonymity.

Her mother tried hard to persuade her to learn a trade. She wanted her to become a dressmaker, but the daughter was not interested. Her drawing alone mattered, and in order to learn more about it she decided to look for work as an artist's model. She had not far to go.

Owing to the presence of the painters, a market for artists' models grew up in the Place Pigalle. The Marché aux Modèles was held on Sundays beside the fountain. It was a loud, crowded market, especially as the Place Pigalle was the terminus of the I and J omnibus routes, the first plying between Pigalle and Les Halles-de-Vins, the second between Montmartre and Pont-Royal. The horse-drawn trams of the La Villette-Trocadéro line added to the din and bustle. The men and women who aspired to earning their living as artists' models arrived on Sunday mornings and waited beside the fountain for the painters to come and choose. You could, André Warnod says in his *Les peintres de Montmartre*, find a model for God the Father or for a *bambino* with golden locks. The café terraces were packed with men in top hats and women in plumes; yellow fiacres passed by, driven by coachmen in white.

The windows of Puvis de Chavannes' vast studio gave onto the square. When Valadon, then fifteen years old, entered the market he asked her to be a model.

Although there would have been nothing out of the ordinary for Puvis' eye to fall on the pretty, intelligent-looking Valadon, she gives a different version of their first meeting. Puvis was one of Madeleine's customers, and Valadon had met him when she delivered his laundry at the studio. Madeleine was a good laundress and had an aristocratic clientele, so it is possible that Puvis was one of her clients, in which case it would have been quite normal for her, unable to afford an errand boy, to send her daughter to deliver his shirts. The first time she went to the studio, Valadon was to relate, Puvis was not there. She found his paint merchant alone and asked him to present her with a few tubes of paint. The man had not the heart to refuse. Then Puvis came in, still in his dress-suit after a long night out, and inquired who she was. He then asked her: "Would you care to pose as St. Geneviève of Paris?"

No matter which version was true, Valadon's answer was an immediate yes. To model for Puvis was a neat stroke of luck. He was famous and, above all, he was rich. With him there was no fear of not being paid or of having to be content with a painting in lieu of cash. Even Renoir would now and then give a painting instead of money. At the end of the first week he engaged her as his permanent model.

Pierre Puvis de Chavannes was tall, bearded and distinguished; he wore a morning coat and black spats and never forgot an insult. In his youth he had been a pupil of Delacroix for a fortnight. During this time Delacroix never spoke a single word to him. In revenge Puvis ran him down for the rest of his life. Puvis was a nobleman: he did not forget that either. He was a man of culture; Virgil was his inspiration. He painted imposing allegorical murals and was a sort of painter-laureate of his day, respected and admired by those in power, loved in the salons and by the mighty, a fervent patriot who had stayed in Paris during the Siege. Both his studios in Pigalle and Neuilly were damaged by the bombardment. In Pigalle two bullets hit a painting, in Neuilly a cannon ball smashed in the roof.

He retained a deep hatred for the Germans; *la revanche* haunted him. Shortly after the war he painted his *Espérance,* a frail girl picking flowers on a battlefield. Until his death he went on patriotic pilgrimages to Versailles. His soul revolted when some French painters consented to hang their pictures in the Berlin Salon. "The place of a Frenchman is in France," he said, "not in foreign countries, especially when the foreign country's aspirations are opposed to those of France."

While Valadon modelled for Puvis and, later on, for Renoir,

she behaved like a quiet, docile girl. Nobody influenced her; the desire to draw came from within. She drew at home, her mother scolding her for wasting her time. In the studios of the Masters she breathed the air that surrounded great painters; she never spoke but listened. Those who knew her in the outside world would not have recognized her. For Puvis she posed as a boy too; her figure allowed it. In the *Bois Sacré*, for instance, the young man who breaks the branch has Valadon's arms and legs. She is also immortalized in Puvis' fresco *Sainte-Geneviève-de-Paris*, in the Panthéon. It was difficult to work for him for he forgot that you were present in the studio, and while he was painting you dared not move.

She was proud of Puvis' friendship and would walk decorously at his side when they went from Neuilly to Pigalle. He spoke in a monotonous voice, not caring whether she listened or not; and she admitted that in fact she never did listen but watched his hands and the way he moved. She did not dare to open her mouth. "I was too respectful for that." Yet if the fancy took her she would say he had been her lover.

Other painters sought her out. Even before she was eighteen, the year she gave birth to her son, she had become Renoir's model. One story has it that Puvis had lent her to Renoir, who then lived on the Butte in the rambling Château des Brouillards. Another story relates that Renoir found her in the model market in the Place Pigalle and was struck by her figure and looks. Be all that as it may, she was the model for the pretty creature in muslin in Renoir's *Danse à la campagne*, and she is in his *Danse à la ville*, wearing an evening frock with train and elbow gloves. One finds her in Renoir's *Baigneuses* too; and when in 1882 Henri de Toulouse-Lautrec visited the International Exhibition at the Georges Petit Gallery and looked at her sleek body in the painting, he could not help observing, "The body of a woman, if it is beautiful, is not made for love. Too good for it. Any wretched body will do for love making." By then Lautrec had met her.

It was he who introduced her to Degas, and though she never modelled for Degas he became for her the most important of the Masters. Degas nicknamed her "the terrible Maria," whereas Lautrec was the one who persuaded her to call herself Suzanne as Marie-Clémentine did not sound like the name of an artist. "So Suzanne has taken the place of Maria," wrote Degas in one of his letters to her. Unfortunately his letters were undated, so they shed no light on the sequence of events. Yet it seems certain that Degas gave her the accolade as an artist some time before her son was born.

Lautrec was the first to see her drawings. He showed them to Fédérigo Zandomeneghi, the painter, and Paul-Albert Bartholomé, the sculptor, who were enchanted by them; they suggested that Degas should see them. Lautrec accompanied her to Degas' studio.

"I sat and listened, very thin yet muscular like a strong young man," she said when recalling that great moment.

Lautrec told her to show Degas her drawings. He looked at them, then at Lautrec, then back at her. "But Maria, Maria," exclaimed Degas, "do you realize that you are one of us?"

"I pressed my hand to my heart," Valadon remembered. "So happy I was, so proud of his praise. Degas wasn't given to praise. He was magnificent but unsociable."

For Valadon, the terrible she-devil Maria, Degas had a deep affection, and he respected her work. He was not usually drawn to women painters: he found their work too genteel and viewed it with a cynical eye. Mary Cassatt was a friend of his, yet once when he looked at a canvas of her as the Virgin holding the Child, he exclaimed: "*Tiens*, little Jesus with his English nurse!"

Degas was an aloof and forbidding man, proud of his noble origin. Edgar de Gas was his real name. He was intolerant with his inferiors, but he accepted Valadon both as a person and an artist. "My dear Maria," he wrote one Sunday, "your letters arrive punctually, your handwriting firm as an engraving. But I see no more of your drawings. I look now and again at the drawing you did with a red pencil, which still hangs in the dining-room, and I say to myself: That diabolic Maria has a genius for drawing."

After her path had moved away from his, and he saw her but seldom, he wrote one day: "Every year, terrible Maria, I see your handwriting executed as if with a saw, but I never see the writer herself with a portfolio under her arm."

It was under his watchful eye that she started engraving. Nobody admired her etchings more than he. "Supple and hard," was his description of them. To Degas she was the one woman who could compete with men.

Whereas Degas was the light and the guide in her development as an artist, Lautrec and his friends opened up new horizons for her by taking her into the world of the Chat Noir of Rodolphe Salis and the Mirliton of Aristide Bruant.

Salis had come to Paris from Picardy. He was thin, pale, and had red hair and a military figure. By profession he was a carver of ecclesiastical statuettes and a painter of popular religious pictures. He established himself in the Boulevard de Rochechouart. He made friends with the poet Émile Goudeau, who, in spite of being shortsighted, never wore glasses because, so he declared, existence was too ugly to be seen at close quarters. With his literary and theatrical friends Goudeau formed a club, where they entertained each other with poems, sketches and songs. They used to meet in the Boulevard Saint-Michel on the Left Bank and called themselves the Hydropathes. Goudeau took his Hydropathes late one night to Salis' workshop, where much wine was drunk and the Hydropathes did their turns. Among the carvings, paintings and stained glass, it was decided to start a cabaret right there on the spot. All they had to do was to repeat the performances they had given and keep them up to date. Thus was born the Chat Noir.

The neighbourhood was a sordid one: on one side of the Chat Noir was the Élysée-Montmartre, a seedy cabaret visited

nightly by crooks, ponces and ruffians; on the other side a row
of prostitutes' hotels; and at the corner of the rue des Martyrs
was La Reine Blanche, a dance hall patronized by harlots and
bad boys. That exquisite world was astonished by the artistic
and intellectual clientele of the Chat Noir. Moreover, the pimps
and ponces could not figure out exactly what went on there
since they were too ignorant and stupid to appreciate its wit and
subtlety. Their antagonism turned into active enmity. Salis
threw out an *apache* who had started a fight in the Chat Noir.
The next night at closing time the bad boys turned up in force.
A fight ensued in the course of which a waiter was murdered.
Salis thought the moment had come to find new premises.

He moved to the rue Victor-Massé with his company, which
included Georges d'Esparbès, Léon Bloy, Émile Goudeau and
Aristide Bruant. The move took place at midnight on July
10, 1885. Salis was dressed as a seventeenth-century nobleman,
the waiters as academicians. They were led by the band of the
Chat Noir playing, as the newspapers reported, on bizarre instruments. Torchbearers marched on each side of the procession,
and the yellow banners of the Chat Noir fluttered in the night
air. Two faithfuls carried an enormous portrait of Salis painted
by Antonio Gandara. Then came men carrying halberds and
harquebuses. Four lackeys brought the sign of the Chat Noir,
a large painting by Adolphe Willette, and they were followed
by a huge crowd and a cortege of carriages. When the procession
reached the new premises Salis broke his sword in two, then
they all partook of an uproarious supper by torchlight, all
very extravagant and exaggerated, yet precisely what the spirit
of Montmartre enjoyed.

Aristide Bruant soon parted from Salis and took over the
evacuated premises of the Chat Noir in the Boulevard de Rochechouart. As he was not a dilettante, the *apaches* did not molest
him. He had come from the provinces like Salis, had left his
native Gatinais to find work in the capital and make his fortune.
It is unnecessary to describe Bruant since Lautrec perpetuated
him on canvas in one of his most often reproduced paintings.

It is so vivid that one cannot imagine Bruant without a wide-brimmed black hat, black cloak and reddish scarf.

Bruant took all sorts of lowly jobs, and while the poor lad nightly roamed the streets of Paris he became aware of his genius; that is, he realized that those streets were his. He transposed the streets into songs, writing the words himself. He grasped the essence of the men and women who flitted about at night in the different parts of Paris. He saw through their lies; their bravado and their poses left him unimpressed, and though he sympathized with them in his poet's heart, his brain did not cease to mock them. In his song *À la Bastoche*, for example, a young braggadocio of the streets, whose only ambition is to cut a fine figure and who has been made desperate by hunger, loses his head and murders the conductor of an omnibus for the sake of the few sous in his ticket machine. He still cuts a fine figure as he puts his head under the blade of the guillotine, and shows the folk of Pantin how bravely a boy of the Bastoche can die.

Bruant used the vocabulary of the underworld for his songs. His *Rose Blanche* still remains the favourite of the Montmartrois.

> *Alle avait, sous sa toque d'martre*
> *Sur la butt' Montmartre,*
> *Un p'tit air innocent;*
> *On l'app'lait Rose, alle était belle,*
> *A sentait bon la fleur nouvelle,*
> *Ru' Saint-Vincent.*

But Bruant was no sentimentalist. In his way he did for the people in the streets what Utrillo was to do for the walls and houses. Bruant became a close friend of Valadon; they were neighbours later in the rue Cortot.

Bruant named his cabaret the Mirliton and then waited for the clients. The clients did not come. The peasant in him raged as he watched the days and weeks go by with heavy expenses and no takings. He was an irascible man, and he was in a specially bad temper one day when his waiter came to the small office where he was stretched out on a sofa nursing his sense of injustice, to tell him that the only client in the bar had complained because there was no music. To add insult to injury the customer was only drinking beer. Bruant jumped up, ran to the bar and hurled all the foul insults he could think of at the customer. Imagining that coarse insults on the part of the management were part and parcel of the entertainment, the customer roared with laughter and then invited Bruant to take a drink with him. After several drinks Bruant sat down at the piano and sang. A few more customers appeared, whom he also insulted wholeheartedly. In short, a good time was had by all and the expenses were nearly covered.

A few nights later the original customer returned with a party of friends. They were received politely.

"What?" asked the disappointed customer. "You don't insult me any more?"

"Is that all you want?" said Bruant thoughtfully. And from that night onward clients were regularly insulted. The Mirliton became a roaring success. When a customer appeared Bruant and his waiters sang in unison:

> *Oh! là, là!*
> *C'tte gueule, c'tte binette!*
> *Oh! là, là!*
> *C'tte gueul' qu'il a!*

When the customer left they had another song ready for him, which stated that all their patrons were pigs.

A grocer in Dieppe came to Paris on a spree and went to the Mirliton. "Here comes another grocer," Bruant shouted insultingly. The man from Dieppe beamed at him. "So you know who I am," he said, gratified.

Years after the Mirliton had closed, a regular patron asked,

"What has become of Bruant?" The patron was King Edward VII.

On the walls of the Mirliton hung paintings by Lautrec, Joseph Bail and Desboutin and sketches by Théophile-Alexandre Steinlen. The price of a small glass of beer, so one reads on a poster by Lautrec, was thirteen sous.

In the Chat Noir Valadon met an insurance clerk called Boissy who was a regular client there and at the Mirliton. Boissy worked at the Abeille insurance company, but he also painted in his spare time. He was an unsuccessful painter, a bad painter, and the son of a drunkard. His mother had committed suicide. Boissy himself was a heavy drinker; in short there was little to recommend him. Yet because she was always fascinated by waifs and strays, Valadon, the disciple and friend of giants like Puvis, Renoir and Degas, became the mistress of the bad painter and alcoholic, and took him back to the rue du Poteau.

The Puny Child

1

VALADON gave birth to a son at 3 rue du Poteau on December 26, 1883, at one o'clock in the afternoon. The street was named after a gibbet that stood there till the end of the eighteenth century. The boy was registered at the Mairie of the 18th *arrondissement* on December 29 under the name of Maurice Valadon. He was illegitimate like his mother. Speculation as to who his father was went on during the whole of his lifetime.

If one had taken a vote on his fatherhood among friends of his mother, Boissy would have received the majority of votes. He was living with Valadon at the time of the boy's birth. When the child was born he celebrated the happy event with libations to "God Pernod," as he put it, yet he refused to adopt him. "It was an impossible situation," Valadon said. "He took it out on me. He was a bad painter, painting pictures no one cared for, so he consoled himself with the bottle and by making awful scenes. Our love didn't last."

Boissy went, but the child remained tied to the skirts of mother and grandmother. "Puny and restless," Valadon described him, "one moment bursting with gaiety, the next moment floundering in despair. We were at our wits' end trying to cheer him up."

"Pale, puny and restless," she repeated whenever she spoke of her son's childhood.

"I heard from Fédérigo Zandomeneghi, my poor Maria," wrote Degas on a Tuesday, "that you were seriously ill after the birth of your son. I insist on reminding you that now that your life is secure you must think only of your work and make full use of your remarkable talent . . ."

The birth of Maurice did not interfere with the remarkable talent. It would have been impossible in the case of so dedicated an artist. Besides, soon after Boissy's departure Henri de Toulouse-Lautrec became Valadon's lover, and he certainly was not the man to stifle her talent.

Lautrec had his studio on the fourth floor of a house in the rue Tourlaque, a steep street off the rue de Caulaincourt. Valadon moved both her mother and son, then about two years old, to the ground floor of the house he lived in. This gives the lie to those who in later years spread the rumour that Valadon neglected her son whenever she had a lover. She was versatile enough to be simultaneously artist, mother and mistress.

Of all her lovers, Lautrec may have matched her best in spite of his extraordinary appearance. He progressed like a huge beetle on three small legs, the third one being his cane. His torso was normal, his beard dark, his lips fleshy and always very wet. He wore a bowler hat, black jacket, black-and-white checked trousers and in winter a blue petersham overcoat with a green scarf. Valadon was able to understand him when he cried out: "To think if only my legs were longer I wouldn't have to paint." And he appreciated her inner strength.

In the rue Tourlaque Valadon also met Henri's father, the

Comte de Toulouse-Lautrec, an amazing eccentric whom his son considered a complete idiot. Admittedly, the Count was a strange person. Up on the Butte, in the Place du Tertre, an equilibrist used to perform on a rope stretched between two roofs. When he crossed the square on the rope he carried a volunteer on his back to the terror of the spectators. The volunteer was his partner. The count paid the rope walker a goodly sum to let him be the volunteer for once, and he was carried across the square on the tightrope. It must have reminded Valadon of her circus days.

While they were together she went every Sunday morning from her flat to Lautrec's studio, where he received his friends around midday. He was one of the first Frenchmen to take to cocktails. He mixed stiff ones, and his visitors departed half drunk from the newfangled concoctions. Every Sunday a cadaverous man entered, carrying a painting under his arm. He sat down in a corner, his canvas beside him, and listened in silence to the conversation. From time to time he turned his painting toward the light in the hope that some one would notice either him or it. No one ever took any notice and after a while he would pick up the canvas and depart. The man was Vincent Van Gogh, who was staying with his brother Théo at 54 rue Lepic, on the Butte. Théo sold paintings for the house of Goupil in the Boulevard de Montmartre.

"All painters are swine," Valadon once muttered, watching Van Gogh slink out of the studio. Then she shouted it aloud. She could be exceptionally noisy when angered or disgusted.

"Ah, that studio in the rue Tourlaque," wrote Gustave Coquiot, the art critic who was to become Valadon's and Maurice's close friend. "How full it was of strange objects; yet the first thing you noticed was the bar, where Lautrec used to mix cocktails for himself and his friends. With him one had to drink steadily. He respected you only if you kept pace with him."

At night Valadon used to go to Lautrec's flat at 19 rue Fontaine, which he shared with a friend called Bourges, a medical student. Léontine, Lautrec's housekeeper, had no bohemian leanings and he enjoyed teasing her.

"Take everything off," he said one evening to Valadon. "I want to see how she reacts to my dining with a naked woman." Valadon stripped, keeping on only shoes and stockings. They sat down to dine; Léontine appeared, recoiled for a second, then served the meal without flinching. However, the next day she complained to Bourges, who repeated her words to Lautrec.

"But Léontine knows what a woman's body looks like," observed Lautrec. "I was fully dressed. I had only taken off my hat."

Neither Valadon nor Lautrec found their affair out of the ordinary. He was not taken aback by her plebeian origin, and she took his deformity in her stride. She was in the full glory of her twenty years, her eyes sparkling, her abundant hair parted in the middle, her neck round and white; yet when Lautrec painted her, and he painted her twice, he erased her youth. The expression is sad, the face pinched and the chin pointed. On the other hand he shows her indomitable will, the will of a man rather than of a woman. She dominated the relationship while it lasted, retaining her liberty, coming and going as the fancy took her, loving or sitting for him only when it suited her. He had no illusions about her.

"She doesn't lack imagination," he said, "and to lie costs her no effort."

Had he wanted to express that in the portraits?

The end was not protracted. On the first floor in the rue Tourlaque lived Gauzi, Lautrec's old friend from Toulouse. He was painting in his flat when Lautrec burst in on him, shouting, "Come at once. Maria wants to kill herself." Gauzi refused to believe him, but Lautrec was so agitated that he rushed with him down to Valadon's flat. The door was ajar; they went in, then both stopped. They heard loud voices in the kitchen. Madeleine, the mother, was upbraiding her daughter.

"You overreached yourself," Madeleine was saying. "You frightened him and he'll never come back."

"He refused to do what I wanted him to do," Valadon said, "so I put on my big act."

"You should have had more patience," said Madeleine.

Followed by Gauzi, Lautrec entered the kitchen and Gauzi asked Valadon: "Why did you make fun of him?" He turned to Lautrec: "My poor friend, she's made a fool of you." Lautrec stared hard at the two women, then he left without saying a word. He did not seek her out again; in fact it was the end between them.

It was a hot summer day in 1901 when Lautrec died. A thunderstorm was approaching and the sickroom suddenly seemed full of flies. Poor Comte de Toulouse-Lautrec tried to catch them, anything to make himself useful. Only a few minutes before the invasion of the flies he had volunteered to cut his dying son's beard. The dying son watched his father chasing the flies.

"*Vieux con*," he suddenly exclaimed. Those were his last words.

Valadon retained her admiration for Lautrec the painter. She put him among her giants, and when he died she cried for weeks —so she said thirty years later.

After Lautrec had parted from her, Valadon, her son and old Madeleine went back to the rue du Poteau. Now Valadon had a new preoccupation, for, surprisingly, she had become ashamed of her son's illegitimacy. "So unlike her," said her friends.

Maurice believed that Boissy was his father in spite of his not living with them any more. But when he was eight years old his mother said to him: "Boissy isn't good enough to be your father; I have found you a more respectable one." It was a queer pronouncement considering that it was Boissy who refused to adopt the boy. The "more respectable one" was Miguel Utrillo y Molins, a native of Barcelona, journalist, painter, man of letters and of some means, who had fallen so deeply in love with the Butte that he lived for a while in the Moulin de la Galette in order to be at the very heart of High Montmartre. He was an admirer of Valadon and she persuaded him to adopt her son.

On April 8, 1891, when Maurice was already eight years old, Miguel Utrillo adopted him. Maurice Valadon thus became Maurice Utrillo at the Mairie of the 9th *arrondissement* because by then Miguel was living in Boulevard de Clichy. Before going to the Mairie, Miguel took drinks in the Café de la Mairie with one Charles Mahaut, who volunteered to go along as a witness. As he could find no other volunteer Miguel took one of the waiters as his second witness.

An unlikely story has it that Valadon had persuaded Miguel to adopt her son in a café, where she told him her sad tale. Asked the Spaniard, "Who was the father?"

"I don't know," she sighed. "It was either Puvis or Renoir."

"I would be proud to sign my name to the work of either artist. Call him Utrillo."

With the putative fathers Valadon was in her element. She told Édouard Herriot, the French statesman, that Maurice's father was a carter whom she had picked up one night in the rue du Poteau; to others she spoke of Puvis and Renoir, but especially of Puvis, who generally kept aloof of women, though he married the Princess Cantacuzena shortly before his death— a purely platonic marriage, an act of gratitude because she had nursed him through an illness. He was hardly the man to fall for his model, yet Valadon calmly declared that he had been her lover and possibly her son's father. "It might have been Puvis," she said. "He was, after all, only sixty years old when Maurice was born."

Maurice did not cherish his new name. By the time he grew up it was to take all Valadon's strength of character and maternal authority to persuade him to sign his canvases Maurice Utrillo and not Maurice Valadon. He compromised by signing himself "Maurice Utrillo V." She got her way only by pointing out that, as she signed her paintings Valadon, it was bound to lead to confusion if he used the same surname. It irked the French boy to have a Spanish father, even though only an adopted one. He always maintained that Miguel, whom he referred to as a Spanish journalist, had only a platonic relationship with his mother. His real father, he stated, was a Frenchman and a Montmartrois like himself. In short, Boissy.

Miguel, however, was eloquently praised for his altruistic act. He was called a true hidalgo, a fine caballero, and an excellent friend. Eventually, he went home to Barcelona, where he married and had two sons.

2

Little Maurice had been adopted but he was not baptized. Valadon was anticlerical, though her anticlericalism was based mostly on superstition, such as the belief that the sight of a monk would bring bad luck or that if a priest came into a home one had to burn sugar when he had gone. Moreover, she called herself a Satanist, meaning only that she was a devilish creature in the sense in which Degas called her the terrible, diabolical Maria. She also considered herself an anarchist.

Practically every day the unbaptized little boy went past the church of Notre-Dame-de-Clignancourt in the Place Sainte-Euphrasie—the square was renamed Place Jules-Joffrin in 1895—which was only a stone's throw from the rue du Poteau. His grandmother often took him inside the church. The old peasant woman remained unaffected by newfangled ideas. She was probably quite ignorant of them. In that cold church, built but two decades before, the small boy saw a statue of Joan of Arc, and his devotion to her lasted till his death.

"I was born near the church of Notre-Dame-de-Clignancourt," he told Gustave Coquiot, the art critic, to whom he spoke freely of his childhood. "That church isn't old or very beautiful, and it stands all alone, but none the less I love it. I painted it especially for *maman*, who still has the painting." Whenever the boy looked up to the hillock he could see on top of it the basilica of the Sacred Heart rising as white as a sugar loaf in neo-Byzantine style, imprisoned by scaffolding. The Sacré-Coeur, too, left a deep impression on him.

Daily Madeleine took him for walks, and it was she who put him to bed at night. She was his constant companion, yet she could not understand him. He was not like other children; certainly not so gay and easygoing as her daughter was at his age. He was moody, too thin and nervous, a precocious child given to making hysterical scenes. She was troubled and worried about him, but she noticed that whenever she gave him *chabrol*—broth laced with red wine—the old-fashioned peasant soup of her native Limousin, the boy calmed down and slept peacefully. When he was in an exceptionally hysterical condition, in her peasant simplicity she increased the quantity of wine, the way Victorian nurses gave spoonfuls of gin to babies to stop their howling. Soon the boy began to insist on more and more wine in his broth. Madeleine never refused it. He was her little lamb who could do whatever he wanted; keeping him quiet and making him happy were her only wishes. Besides, *faire chabrol* was a normal Limousin custom and thousands of children partook of it without harm.

Valadon's attitude toward little Maurice was similar to that of the grandmother. It is not easy for a creative artist to be an all-round mother. She was too involved in her work to be able to give the complete attention a problem child like Maurice expected, and so she solved her problem by spoiling him or delegating authority to Madeleine, who spoiled him perhaps even more. Maurice quickly learnt that if he wanted anything, all he had to do was to wax hysterical. What he seemed to want most was a good dose of wine in his broth.

The first school Utrillo went to was an elementary school in the Place Saint-Pierre. His grandmother or a servant girl would walk with him to school through the badly paved streets, where grass grew between the cobbles, chickens scratched and pecked, the cows lowed in their stalls. "One did not 'sacré-coeur' yet on the still empty Butte," sang Bruant of the Montmartre of Utrillo's childhood.

Utrillo kept apart from other children and was as moody at school as he was at home. During playtime he did not join in but sat alone, lost in gloomy reverie. If the other children disturbed him or, thinking that the quiet boy was asleep, tried to play some prank on him, he threw himself at them with great violence. He was always the loser.

He was not spared any humiliating prank or cruel trick that boys can devise. His mother gave him a white beret which he wore on a Sunday for the first time. In the square several boys were playing, some belonging to his school. They called him over and he went up to them unsuspectingly. They seized him, tore the beret off his head, threw it into the mud, then fished it out and kicked it about, playing football with it. He cried, imploring them to return the beret, but they were merciless. When they had ruined it completely they threw it into a tree, where it remained.

"A strange child," said his schoolmasters.

Valadon took him from the elementary school and sent him to the Institut Flaisselle in the rue Labat, a private school frequented by middle-class children, hoping that in the more genteel environment Maurice's life would be easier. None the less the fights and beatings and misery continued there.

Valadon drew her small son taking a foot bath. The expression of the thin, naked boy is far from amiable. Nothing seems to amuse him and he appears to dislike people. In short, not a child one would open one's arms to or try to play with. Yet he is a distinguished-looking child with delicate features. She made another drawing of the servant girl taking him to school. He wears a beret; his satchel hangs on a strap from his shoulder. One sees only a back view of him, yet one feels, as he walks along

with his head down, that he is not happy. The servant girl
looks at him obviously without pleasure.

3

Utrillo was taken out of the private school when Paul Mousis established himself in his mother's life. Mousis is a ghostlike
figure. He somehow has no substance, though he was a man
of substantial means. He is an improbable apparition in Valadon's life, for there had been nobody like him before, and no
one even faintly resembling him came after. She met Mousis
through Erik Satie, the composer, when she was painting his portrait in oils. That was in 1893. She became Mousis' mistress in
the same year.

Paul Mousis belonged to a rich bourgeois family. He was a
partner in the firm of Bel et Sainbenat, a big business firm in
Paris. Practically every writer and art critic who wrote of Valadon said that she married Mousis but that was not so. Apparently none of them took the trouble to write to the Mairie of
Bessines and ask for her birth certificate for they never married.

In 1896 she gave up modelling and, like any other suburban
wife, went to live with Mousis at Pierrefitte-Montmagny. Valadon, who had rubbed shoulders with the *lorettes*, remained
with Mousis for sixteen long years, until she was forty-five.

Mousis was agreeable to having Utrillo living with them. In
any case she would not have gone without him. Son, mother
and grandmother went to the comfortable suburban house, a
strikingly different world from the one left behind in the rue du
Poteau. Yet it made little difference to Utrillo. He remained morose and restless, always ready to make a scene if he did not
have his way. The comfort and financial security of Mousis'
house did not attract or affect him. He led his life as though
he were still in the old home in the rue du Poteau. Mousis treated
the boy kindly and well, and received little gratitude in return.
For Utrillo, one was either a friend or an enemy—he decided in-

stinctively and often incorrectly. In spite of everything Mousis did for him, he remained an enemy.

Montmagny lies between Deuil and Pierrefitte in the department of Seine et Oise. Ugly blocks of flats have been raised since Mousis' day, yet one can still find streets with slate-roofed houses, trying to be small replicas of bourgeois country residences. One feels that the owners refer to their rose bush as the rose garden and to their apple tree as the orchard. Mousis built his house on the road to Groslay near the vineyards of the Butte-Pinson.

Today no vineyards remain on the slopes of the Butte-Pinson. Pylons converge on the hill as if they hold their yearly convention there. When Mousis took Valadon and Utrillo into his house the hill was still dotted with taverns and *guinguettes,* not the best neighbourhood for the boy.

Valadon settled down to country life. Those who knew her in her Montmagny days said she spent her time like any country woman—when she was not in Montmartre, that is. Mousis had the ground-floor flat at 12 rue Cortot. She would come to Paris in style, driving a mule, her five Alsatians running and gambolling beside the light carriage. In the Montmagny garden she kept a hind. In the rue Cortot there was a garden which she decided to turn into a zoo—nothing dangerous, as the wild beasts consisted only of the hind and afterward a goat. In his middle-class fashion Mousis admired and encouraged her eccentricities and probably boasted of them to his business friends.

The growing boy was sent to the Collège Rollin, now the Lycée Jacques Decour, in the Avenue Trudaine in Paris. On weekday mornings he was given money for his daily fare from Montmagny to the Gare du Nord and back. When he returned in the evenings he was usually in a dark and difficult mood, which frightened his grandmother. It took her a long time to perceive that the boy was heavy with drink. She could not be blamed for her slow perception, for getting drunk is hardly one of the things expected from a schoolboy. If his grandmother upbraided him he shouted her down, tore off his collar, tipped up his exercise books and so upset the poor, simple old woman that she meekly put him in bed and then gave him a plateful of her broth.

On his way from the Collège Rollin to the Gare du Nord, Utrillo often fell in with the *maraîchers*—market gardeners—from Montmagny, who drove home at that hour in their huge, two-wheeled covered carts. They would give him a lift back, and so Utrillo saved the return fare. He spent the money on drink with some of his schoolmates before joining the *maraîchers*, who in their turn stopped at several inns on the road. They took the boy in with them and gave him absinthe or wine. Hence his drunken return to Mousis' country house.

There is, as one would expect, another version, namely that the men who took him home were quarry men. Their carts were open, so in winter the poor boy shivered in the cart while the quarry men caroused in the warm taverns. However, they were not hardhearted and eventually took pity on the boy, brought him inside and all drank merrily together. Probably both versions were true.

The boy's thirst grew and drinking with schoolmates and travel companions was no longer enough for him.

"Give me the bottle," he shouted to his trembling grandmother.

She said there was no bottle. She had locked the Pernod away.

"Give it me or I'll break up everything," he threatened.

He always got his way with his grandmother. And she would not "sneak" on him but put him to bed before Mousis returned from his office in Paris. When Mousis stayed at home, she kept the boy away from him. Utrillo remained as spoiled and willful in Montmagny as he had been in Montmartre.

His drinking with market gardeners or quarry men is part and parcel of the legend that grew up around Maurice Utrillo. For schoolboys to take *apéritifs* sounds almost unbelievable, yet it was true. One of his schoolmates who turned into a pompous government official was always ready to confirm it. He lived on the Butte and was known as "Le Temps," not after the weather but the newspaper of that name which was considered highbrow and which he carried with him as a symbol of his admirably cultured mind. "Le Temps" was a short man, usually dressed in a brown corduroy suit with an imposing black hat. He had a fawn-coloured moustache, worked in some office in Paris and came back on the *funiculaire* in the evening, the newspaper, naturally, under his arm. He reached the Place du Tertre, stopped in the middle of the square and unfolded the paper. He read with deep concentration for a few minutes, then carefully folded it and made for one of the many bistro-cum-restaurants in the square. He came to a sudden halt before entering the bar, the newspaper was unfolded again, and his head and large hat disappeared behind it. There must have been something of urgent importance he had forgotten to read and which brooked no delay. That usually took place in the doorway. In the bistro he liked reminiscing of his schooldays at the Collège Rollin.

"I was with Maurice there," he would say. "We went to the Café des Oiseaux in the Place d'Anvers, next door to the school." The café is still next to the school. "We took our *apéritifs* in the café. Of course, never in the morning, only in the evening when the day's work was done. We were a merry crowd, Maurice the least merry of us, though he could at times be very noisy. Then his mother took him away from the college."

When he was asked whether Utrillo got drunk as a schoolboy, "Le Temps" replied, "He gave the impression that he was born drunk." Then taking his newspaper he would leave the bistro and walk sedately home, the responsible civil servant that he was. To him, the *apéritifs* had done no harm.

But to Utrillo, they had. The thousands of Limousin children who drank *chabrol* grew up without any aftereffect. The boys of the Collège Rollin who frequented the Café des Oiseaux could evolve into men like "Le Temps." Yet with Utrillo that

was not the case. He had become a confirmed alcoholic well before he reached maturity. One could speculate on the reasons,
trying to find one explanation. Yet there are many: Boissy
was an alcoholic and many writers considered the trait to be inherited; Utrillo's willfulness as a small child was allowed to go
uncurbed; Utrillo's strange environment in the rue du Poteau
with a temperamental mother and a doting, simple grandmother;
the insecurity of their finances before wealthy Mousis came
along; and Utrillo's antisocial attitude and fundamental sadness.
All were frustrations to which drink provided an outlet. One
must also add that Mousis' presence during the formative
years might have made the boy envious, frustrated in his deep
love for his mother.

Whichever may be the right answer, probably all of them, the
fact remains that at the mere age of sixteen, Utrillo was a hard-
ened alcoholic.

Valadon and Mousis had hoped that the Collège Rollin would
turn Utrillo into a nice, decent, industrious, middle-class boy
who would in time pass his *baccalauréat* and then go on to the
Sorbonne. But Utrillo was not industrious and had no staying
power. He succeeded in making progress only in mathematics.
In the classroom he was docile and respectful; after school it
was a different matter. He reached home later and later. Mousis
thought the boy was wasting his time at the college. Valadon
agreed and Utrillo was taken away. Valadon still tried to believe
that there was nothing fundamentally wrong with her son. She
refused for a long time to bracket him with the unbalanced and
the hopeless alcoholics. The college, she felt sure, had been a bad
influence on her Maurice. Now everything would be perfect.

Mousis said what the boy needed was a job. Let him have a
job. There followed a series of jobs; he never stayed long in
any of them. One of the first was with Dufayelle, an empo-
rium that specialized in cheap furniture. It had a vast provincial
clientele, and Utrillo was employed to write the addresses on

the catalogues the firm sent out all over France. His handwriting was atrocious, especially when he was in his cups, and he got his addresses wrong. He was fired.

His next employer was a milliner for whom he carried hat-boxes around Paris. Though the milliner was Valadon's personal friend, Maurice had to give up the hatboxes, for there were too many opportunities to drop in at bistros. Other jobs of short duration followed. He was employed by a shoe-cream manufacturer, then in a lamp-shade factory. A publicity agency came after that, and he even worked as a mason's apprentice in Saint-Denis. The smell of plaster nauseated him—one more reason to drink heavily. He lost his jobs either because he had fights with his colleagues, turned up drunk or failed to turn up at all. Nothing lasted longer than a month.

At one of his jobs he sided with an apprentice whom some workmen were bullying. One day when the workmen were especially nasty to his colleague, Utrillo bravely flew at them. In the the ensuing fight the workmen grabbed Utrillo, pushed him into a dustbin, and stood round laughing and jeering.

"In that dustbin I decided never to become a socialist," was his comment when he spoke of the occasion.

A friend of Mousis found him employment in the Crédit Lyonnais. He was made a cashier. At that time rakes were used, since payment was mostly made in gold coins. One day a client appeared, a short, fat, rich man, wearing a brown bowler hat, the badge of the French *rentier*. Cashier Utrillo eyed the man for a while, then down came the rake on the bowler hat. There was a terrible scene and Utrillo was immediately fired.

"It was his instinctive revolt against the rich, the bohemian rising up against the bourgeois," his mother interpreted.

The truth was far more humdrum. First, Utrillo was not a cashier at the Crédit Lyonnais, and second, he was employed only for twenty days, from June 5 to June 25, in the year 1900. One became a cashier in that bank only after many years of service, and the idea of a youth of seventeen holding such a position

makes any banker smile. Utrillo was a sort of apprentice office
boy. He simply ceased to put in an appearance.

Who gave birth to the story of the brown bowler hat? It
could only have been Valadon, the great mystifier, the spinner
of tales. In her native Limousin the peasants used to gather in
some barn on the eve of a feast or the harvest or some simi-
larly important event, or at the home of the deceased during a
wake, and *les conteurs de veillées,* men with imagination, entertained the assembly. She would have been a success among
them, outdoing all the rest. The truth was too drab; to lose a
job because of a hangover too prosaic; so she invented the brown
bowler and the rake.

Utrillo had his own story about his brief spell in the Crédit
Lyonnais.

"I was employed in one of the branches," he told Gustave
Coquiot during one of their long chats. "I was a surprising bookkeeper. I continued to drink while working there, arriving in
the mornings like the terror among ledgers and figures and
pass books and all other complications of banking."

The jobs came to an end; Utrillo stayed at home in Montmagny, drinking heavily. He was infinitely clever in obtaining
drink. "There were no depths to which my son wouldn't sink
when in search of drink," Valadon said. He frequented the taverns and *guinguettes* of the Butte-Pinson. He had fights and
rows, and the peasants and workmen who spent their Saturday
evenings and Sunday afternoons on the hill came to dislike him.
Yet at the same time they could not refrain from filling him up
with drink in order to make a fool of this youth of eighteen.

When Utrillo got an idea into his head he worried it as a
dog gnaws a bone. In his cups he invented elaborate practical
jokes to play on the peasants, but before he could put them into
execution his boon companions would beat him up. The overexcited, gesticulating Parisian was just the target for them. Valadon was in despair, and Utrillo, who loved his mother to the
point of adoration, cried and promised to mend his ways. Then

he would meet a tavern acquaintance and drop back into the dark gulf of drink. Drink gave him no comfort. In the evening he would reappear at home with bruised lips and black eyes.

Eventually, Mousis noticed Utrillo's drinking—it could no longer be hidden from him. He urged Valadon to take her son to Sainte-Anne, the lunatic asylum and hospital for nervous diseases in the rue Cabanis near the Santé prison. The asylum stands in a pleasant park; trees line the drive, and the different buildings do not look grim if you are only visiting. Valadon took her son only for a medical consultation; she wanted to find out how he could be weaned from drink at home. To her surprise and grief the doctors decided to keep him. She argued with them but they were adamant: if she wanted him cured he would have to stay at Sainte-Anne for two months. The youth of eighteen remained, the mother went home. Valadon felt a little more cheerful because her son would completely be cured and the nightmare of his drinking would come to an end.

The Painter
in Spite of Himself

1

*V*ALADON maintained that Renoir, Degas and Lautrec—in
short, her "giants"—had not influenced her drawing and
painting. However, she had learnt from them the art of self-
dedication. They were men who took their painting not only
seriously but considered it of vital importance to mankind, a
victory over the Philistines, a war constantly waged against
the ugly and retrograde. Their mission, those painters felt, was
to open man's eyes to the true scale of values. Though less interested in mankind as a whole, Valadon followed their example.
Her art came first.

   She considered painting inseparable from life. "I paint with
the stubbornness I need for living, and I've found that all
painters who love their art do the same." Degas impressed her
more by his gift of observation than by his aesthetic theories. To
render intensively some aspect of life was almost an act of faith
with her.

In the rue Tourlaque and in Montmagny she mostly drew and etched. In 1892 she painted an unflattering self-portrait. In the pursuit of her aim to render intensively some aspect of life, there was no room for flattery. While she watched her giants at work she had observed that they were never unfaithful to their technique, but kept rigorously within its bounds; in fact their creative power was shackled to it. To move beyond it, they knew, would break up the concept of the whole. You construct well only with material which you can handle and which is within your reach. Valadon, young as she was then, was already aware of the material. For her everything had to be harsh and hard. She wanted nothing pretty in her domain. "I paint people," she said, "because I want to know them. Don't bring women to me who want something pleasant or pretty. I'd only disappoint them."

Her women had to be plain, ordinary women, preferably from the working class. They were usually heavily built and neither smiled nor tried to look pleased with life. Valadon searched for simple subjects which her genius could amplify. In her drawings and etchings those squat, dumpy women and unsmiling, little boys have a strength that her intensity alone could give them. Yet they remain earthy.

She drew them washing themselves, taking baths, in short when they had no chance to strike a figure or show off. A person in the act of washing his body reveals his least artificial self. With Valadon, eye and technique worked together. If one thinks of technique, one should, as a striking example, compare her women with those of Matisse.

When there is no admiring beholder present the naked body is stripped of self-consciousness and, so Valadon observed, the act of ablution becomes serious work. Those women washing themselves are preoccupied: they even frown. Did I forget to wash under my armpits? Have I dried my legs properly? Did I wet my hair? Valadon records those questions. The rooms where her women and children bend over, sit, squat or rise, are like cells, the walls bare, the furniture heavy and the towels frayed. You are struck by Valadon's deep knowledge, not so much of the world as of life; everything is supple and hard, as Degas put it.

She was seldom satisfied with her work. *"Mon Dieu,* what a little masterpiece," she said one moment. "It should have been better," she said a moment later. "One can surely express oneself better." She was in continuous pursuit of the completeness she longed for and the perfection that happily one never reaches, for once an artist has found perfection he has nothing left to pursue. The chase lasted until her death.

She etched on soft-ground, *vernis mou.* The process was no longer fashionable: the second half of the eighteenth and the first half of the nineteenth century had been its heyday. Artists like Gainsborough, Bonington, Turner, Decamps and Royss had made frequent use of it. Soft-ground etching gives a much softer print than ordinary etching, yet Valadon surprised everyone, including Delâtre, her printer, with the violence of her line. The zinc plates, which were of ordinary plumber's zinc, were badly varnished and she let the acid bite deeply into the plate. "It differs superbly from the usual, bloodless soft-ground etching," remarked Delâtre, after he had overcome his astonishment.

"Her work is always outstanding," Berthe Weill, an art dealer, was to say of her. "Many run her down because she makes no concessions. That is her great merit. A great artist."

Francis Jourdain, the writer and art collector, frequented Lebarc's art gallery in the rue Le Peletier. In 1892 Lebarc organized an exhibition of impressionists and symbolists. He showed to Jourdain the Valadon drawings which he was including in the exhibition.

"Not bad, eh?" Lebarc said. "They're by a little artist's model . . . She has never been taught . . . Watching one of her employers, she had the idea to try her hand. Very gifted, isn't she? One would hardly think that they are drawn by a woman."

The employer, Lebarc added, was Degas.

Jourdain was struck by her draughtsmanship. She evaded no problem but drew with courage and obstinacy which showed her strong personality and almost cruel preoccupation with truth. She was then twenty-seven years old.

Her first private exhibition was at the Société Nationale des Beaux-Arts in 1894. Then came a long absence from the *galeries* which lasted until 1909. She sold her work in the interval through Lebarc and Vollard, and also through some very minor dealers.

At the time when Utrillo returned from the asylum of Sainte-Anne she was already a mature painter in so far as her art was balanced, her technique completely developed; in simple words, she knew where she was going. This was of immense importance for the next move in her son's life.

2

When Utrillo was taken away from the Collège Rollin, Mousis had threatened him with a reformatory school if he did not look for a job. Utrillo looked for jobs, found jobs and lost every one. The next move was Sainte-Anne. Now, he was back from Sainte-Anne; what could one do with or for him? To send him job hunting was out of the question. He was not cut out for jobs and a young man of his age could no longer be threatened with reformatory school. Neither Valadon nor Mousis could think of a solution.

Utrillo was docile, obedient and quiet. The cure appeared to have worked. He had no desire to drink, but, as Valadon could not help observing, he had lost all his vitality. He stood for hours at the window, drumming on the pane, his eyes on the houses, the street and the trees, though not on the shapes that came and went in the street. His drumming irritated his mother, but apart from that she thought that everything was perfect in the garden.

Neither mother nor son belonged to any world, society or class. They were free, as it were, of a sense of social duty or any other sort of obligations. Money for them was a matter of luck: they were in luck now because Mousis had lots of it—tomorrow he and the money might vanish. Still, life would go on, so why worry? With this mentality it is not surprising that Valadon accepted her son's indolent existence.

Utrillo occasionally wrote poetry, atrociously bad poetry; he read articles in *La Croix*, a militant Catholic paper, and saw himself as a mystic; he read scientific books without understanding them, yet believed he could be a scientist. He immersed himself in trashy blood-and-thunder stories, then went back to the window and drummed on the pane. He too had accepted the new existence. His behaviour was generally shy and humble, though there were sudden gusts of temper followed by scenes, but nothing really to worry about. Valadon drew and painted, her son was home, and she saw no reason to think beyond that. However, Mousis did. With his middle-class background and essence, he perceived that something was very wrong. For a young man of nineteen to be lazing around, accepting such an empty life went against his beliefs and tenets. He persuaded Valadon to go to see a doctor.

She chose a Dr. Ettlinger for whom she had once made some furniture. Working in oak, she designed and carved furniture using only a saw, chisel and hammer. The doctor had bought two armchairs from her for his drawing room. She took Utrillo to him.

"Find an outlet for his overexcitement," the doctor said. "He is a bundle of nerves. Take the young man out of himself. You are a painter so give him a pencil or even a brush. Why not give him a taste for painting?"

Valadon was not impressed. Painting was too sacred to be used as occupational therapy. It was a vocation and a gift. Her son had seen her drawing and painting ever since he was a toddler without taking the slightest interest. He hardly glanced at her work.

"This young man is approaching twenty," the doctor went on. "There are no signs of dementia, but his behaviour is infantile. He is incapable of any sustained effort, and there are a thousand reasons to fear a relapse into his old vice. You should persuade him to occupy himself with painting since you are a painter yourself."

Valadon promised she would try and left it at that. Not so Mousis who insisted on her also seeing Dr. Vallon, who was Utrillo's doctor at Sainte-Anne. Dr. Vallon told her that if nothing were done to keep her son occupied, he could easily relapse in spite of the rigorous treatment he had undergone in the mental hospital. She should find him something to do. She was a painter; why not interest him in painting? She should make an effort and give him a few lessons. This time Valadon was a little more impressed.

Utrillo was furious when she spoke to him. He made a scene, shouting that he had not the slightest intention to learn to paint. He had never held a brush in his hand, he had never looked at a painting, and it was ridiculous to want to interest him in it. He was satisfied with the life he led, he did not drink, so why annoy him? Why make him do something he did not care for? But at last impressed by medical opinion, Valadon did not give in. She threatened to send him back to Sainte-Anne if he did not comply.

"I started to paint to please my mother," Utrillo said, looking back on his beginnings as a painter.

The woman who had never taken lessons now began to instruct her son in the art of painting. He was incredibly lucky there, for she put at his disposal not only her own knowledge of painting but all she had seen and observed in the studios of her giants. André Warnod, who like several other Montmartre writers first set out to become a painter, has described the studios and academies of art at the turn of the century. One studio he frequented was that of Jules Lefebre in the rue Fromantin. The models were icily immobile and overprofessional. One started with the head on Monday and finished with the feet on Saturday; and woe to those who did not keep to the rules. The studio produced a number of Prix de Rome winners. Utrillo was saved from such a fate by his mother. He would never have had the patience and industry to stick to such an establishment.

The two doctors had suggested painting only because Valadon *was* a painter. Had she been a breeder of dogs they would have advised her to interest her son in dogs. What the doctors did not know and could not know was that Valadon's total devotion to art would extend to the lessons she gave her son—she put all her strength, talent and enthusiasm into them. It was no longer a question of keeping him occupied; it was a challenge to implant her own dedication, skill and sureness of technique to Utrillo—a far cry from the doctors' intentions.

It was an uphill fight. Utrillo would work a little one day and rebel the next. Painting meant nothing to him—he merely feared being sent back to Sainte-Anne and so he plodded on without joy or conviction. The tall, dark-haired, young man with pale-blue eyes would sit dejected on a window-sill, stirring colours with his brush, staring out through the open window, trying to put on cardboard (he wasn't given canvas) the line of the horizon above the hill and the cottages among the trees.

He complained of strange noises in his head when he painted. Now and then he threw the brushes away, screaming that he had had enough of them. But his mother insisted on his going on. It irked her to see him taking her sacred art so disdainfully, yet she did not give up. "No artist," said Adolphe Tabarant, the famous art critic who was to write a book on Utrillo, "has shown himself as uninterested in his vocation as Utrillo, who came to it by way of medicine without the slightest zest or sympathy."

It went on during the whole summer of 1902. Utrillo lounged about, hands in trouser pockets, his mouth half open, looking like an imbecile. He made little effort; starting, then stopping, dabbling rather than working.

"Maurice," she said, "don't daydream. Paint." This was the mother speaking.

Maurice would come to her with his latest effort. "Just look at this," Valadon exhorted him. "You tried to paint a street, but a street rises. Yours doesn't. You have to learn that streets rise and roofs slope." That was the painter speaking.

He started again and slowly his mother's words began to sink in. Perspective and angles became his constant preoccupation when working on a landscape. "Watch your angles," his mother said when looking at his efforts.

Valadon gave Utrillo her painter's palette with her favourite five colours: two chrome yellow, one vermilion, one deep red and one zinc white. She let him use them in his own fashion. On his occasional trips to Paris he had seen paintings by Sisley and Pissarro in the windows of the Durand-Ruel Gallery. Sisley impressed him most, and he tried to follow his style. Now and again he thought that he painted like Pissarro.

"If I thought it was good, I asked: 'Is it like Sisley, *hein?*' Why Sisley? I saw nothing by that master, but my mother spoke of him, so I repeated the name. One is stupid, isn't one, when one begins?"

He said that to Coquiot when he was already sure of himself as a painter. Like his mother he was an expert at twisting the past. You have only to look at his short impressionist period to see Sisley's influence.

He began to take an interest in painting. Then came the great day which neither he nor his mother expected. She looked at a landscape he had just finished and was astounded by the sureness of his eye and sense of perspective. "You've done that like a painter," she said, delighted. "All you need now is to learn to draw." She let him take her easel when he went out to paint. The days of the window-sill were over.

"One more piece of advice," she said to him. "No painter

ever existed who painted as he wished. Every painter paints as he sees the objects he intends to paint; in short, he paints as he can."

In spite of his veneration for his mother and the lessons she had given him, Utrillo did not try to imitate her, and, Sisley or no Sisley, he went instinctively for his own target as if he knew that there was a form of painting which was his alone. Of course, it was no easy sailing. He dirtied the palette, the colours were applied too heavily, and he waxed furious, remembering how easy it had looked in the windows of Durand-Ruel. His mother watched over him, explaining how to improve his work. She spoke to him as one painter to another. Occupational therapy was over: only the painter remained.

Here one cannot help asking the question: Would Utrillo have become a painter if the two physicians had not suggested this therapy? The "ifs" of life and history are but a matter of speculation or food for reverie, yet it seems likely that if he had been the son of a bookkeeper and a cook he would not have become a painter. Theirs was a happy combination in so far as Valadon was the seed and he, the rich, fertile soil. Even the best soil if left fallow yields nothing and if the soil is not rich the seed is wasted. One could add that before genius manifests itself a period of incubation is needed. It is like children hearing words they cannot understand. Utrillo had seen his mother's paintings ever since he was born, and he grew up beside a woman for whom art came before everything else. That must have sunk in, even if only unconsciously. When he stood drumming on the windowpane, staring into nothingness, he soaked in the street, walls and trees, and when Valadon had forced him to paint, the street, walls and trees reappeared on the canvas, basking in the light of his colossal talent.

"If his mother hadn't forced him to paint he would probably have died quite young in some asylum," was the two doctors' opinion. Wasted, like champagne gone flat, one could add.

The happy mother gave her son more and more freedom. He

set up his easel at street corners or in the countryside, and the peasants and boon companions of yore were surprised to see him taking his work seriously.

"Eh, Maurice," they said, "you've become a painter now?"

Utrillo nodded and went on painting. Butter would not have melted in his mouth. And Mousis of all people was impressed by his work. That shadowy figure about whom so little is known had a feeling for painting, and he took some of Utrillo's landscapes to his partners in the rue Bourdaloue. For a beginner they brought a handsome price. Framed, the landscapes hung in the partners' offices, the first walls to be graced by Utrillo's pictures. "That one has done nothing for me either," Utrillo complained of Mousis. He must have forgotten his first sale.

Valadon was happy. Her Maurice had found his vocation and there would be no more trouble with drink. He was a normal person with an aim in life. If you love, you believe, and look neither under the carpet nor into the corners. She did not, therefore, attach any importance to his singular attitude toward women. He shunned their company, not like a misogynist, but like an adolescent who thinks that skirts are stupidly ridiculous and knickers obscene. The doctors had said he was immature, and nothing showed his immaturity more than in his relations, or rather lack of relations, with women. At puberty a boy becomes frightened of women. The kiss of the dear lady who is a friend of his mother turns into a sort of bodily contact which the boy finds repulsive. But then, time, the great healer, begins to operate and what time and opportunity do not achieve, schoolmates do. French schoolboys are not the bashful kind; they talk freely of sex. Though Utrillo was always willing to drink with them, he kept aloof from his schoolmates and did not share their fun. To quote "Le Temps" again, he became furious when the others giggled about sex. Sex meant women and the only women in Utrillo's life were his mother and grandmother, whom he valued as much as he did Joan of Arc. Utrillo

Maurice Utrillo as a young boy, with his mother Suzanne Valadon.

"Montmartre Cancans" and *Poème satirique* by Maurice Utrillo. In the background, right, the Moulin de la Galette.

A photograph of Maurice Utrillo, taken shortly after his rise to fame as a painter.

Portrait of Edgar Degas by Marcellin-Gilbert Desboutin.

Amedeo Modigliani.

Henri de Toulouse-Lautrec.

"Nude," crayon drawing by Suzanne Valadon.

"Nu à l'éponge," drawing by Suzanne Valadon (1892).

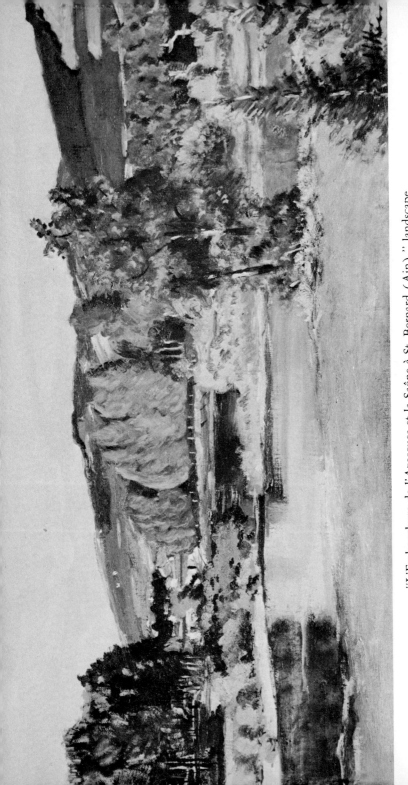

"L'Embouchure de l'Azergues et la Saône à St. Bernard (Ain),'' landscape painting by André Utter.

A postcard of the Impasse Traînée on the Butte-Montmartre that belonged to Utrillo. There are small holes at the corners where Utrillo has pinned up the postcard prior to painting. He originally thought of painting the Impasse without snow and wrote *"Pas de Neige"* on the postcard, then changed his mind, crossing *"Pas de"* and leaving *"Neige."*

One of the paintings that resulted from the above—complete with snow.

"Portrait de Maurice Utrillo" by Suzanne Valadon (oil, 1921).

"Église de Rouvray (Côte d'Or)" by Maurice Utrillo (oil, 1925).

"Château de St. Bernard (Ain)" by Maurice Utrillo (gouache, 1927).

Je soussigné Maurice UTRILLO , certifie que le tableau dont la
photographie est ci-contre , n'est pas une oeuvre de moi .

PARIS, le 21 Janvier 1949

Reproduction of a fake Utrillo, together with his note to certify it is not by
him.

Lucie Valore, Utrillo and caged bird at Le Vésinet

Utrillo as an old man at Le Vésinet.

took the conversations of his schoolmates and later of the peasants on the Butte-Pinson as direct insults to them. His mother was the finest person in the world—it was the other women who indulged in dirt.

Valadon convinced herself that his infantile attitude toward women would vanish in the same way as his craving for drink. Painting would take care of that too. Painting had become the panacea to all Utrillo's ills.

She went to see Dr. Vallon, to whom she showed a folder full of her son's drawings. The doctor was much impressed by the drawings and expressed the opinion that Utrillo's freedom of movement could be restored. The best thing, the doctor thought, was to take him back to Montmartre, where in any case Valadon now spent most of her time.

Utrillo had turned into a handsome young man and had grown a beard. His proud mother took him to Montmartre, where she installed him in Mousis' flat in the rue Cortot in the very center of the Butte. The son of Montmartre, as Utrillo liked to refer to himself, was back in his native land. He was twenty-three years old.

3

When Utrillo reappeared in Montmartre, the finest period of the Butte had already begun. One could not say people were coming from the four corners of the world to watch the spectacular dawn breaking, but they came from all the regions of France, drawn by the spirit's sweet piping. A few came from Italy, a strong contingent from Spain, and there was to be art, music, literature, drunkenness, song, fame, fornication and suicide galore. The spirit of Montmartre must have danced many a *pas seul* in the first decade of the century.

The chroniclers of those halcyon days—Francis Carco, Pierre Mac Orlan, Roland Dorgelès and André Warnod—recorded the creative art, wine, women, song, elaborate practical jokes and very little else. However, that was not the whole picture. A large working-class population had grown up on the sacred mountain. The clash between workmen and bohemians became inevitable. When, at six in the morning, the workmen going to work met the artists swaggering home drunk, relations between the two groups worsened. There were endless sharp battles; workmen were more muscular than artists. Utrillo was probably the one who suffered the most at the workmen's hands. They were the last people to understand or appreciate him.

During Utrillo's absence a lot had changed. The Chat Noir was no longer: Rodolphe Salis had died in 1897. Bruant had tired of the Mirliton and of singing and insulting. The clown Fernando-Boum-Boum was at the height of his fame in the Cirque Médrano. At the Divan Japonais the *pièce de résistance* was Le Coucher d'Yvette, and the Élysée-Montmartre was losing its clients to the Moulin Rouge.

A man known as Père Salz had opened a small cabaret named À Ma Campagne in the rue des Saules in High Montmartre near to the rue Cortot, where Utrillo took up residence with his mother. However, in the rue Saint-Vincent a tavern had opened that was also called À Ma Campagne. Père Salz changed the name of his cabaret to the blood-curdling Cabaret des Assassins, and in order to impress the bourgeois clientele that came to the Butte on Sunday, in the saloon he hung up a knife which he soaked daily in blood supplied by the butcher. With that knife, he explained to his horror-stricken audience, Tropmann, the notorious murderer, had cut the throats of a whole family. Now and then the cabaret was to live up to its new name.

André Gill, the painter and sketcher, often visited the Butte. He was the natural son of a dressmaker, Adeline Gosset, and the Comte de Guines. He chose Gill as his pseudonym; his first drawings appeared in *Le Journal Amusant*. One evening when he was drinking with his friend Émile Goudeau in the Cabaret des Assassins Père Salz asked him to paint a sign for the cabaret.

Gill complied. The sign represented a rabbit escaping from a casserole. People looked at the sign and said: *"Voici le lapin à Gill,"* for Gill was a famous artist by then. The constant repetition of *lapin à Gill* gave the cabaret its third and final name: the Lapin Agile—appropriate enough, since a rabbit has to be pretty agile to be able to escape from a casserole.

Gill had painted the sign in 1890. In the following year he became insane and was locked up in the asylum for incurable mental patients at Charenton. He spent the remaining four years of his unhappy life bragging about his millions, his carriage and servants. "One takes off one's hat before the dead," he said to a man who was staring at him through the bars.

One day the Lapin's sign mysteriously disappeared. Nobody had any idea who could have taken it or where it had gone. Long after it had been given up for lost, it was found in the flat of Tabarant, the distinguished art critic and writer. No questions were asked and the sign was brought back to the rue des Saules.

After Père Salz's death Francis Jourdain, the writer and art collector, had begun to frequent the Lapin, which was to become a home away from home to Utrillo. It was kept by a woman called Adèle assisted by one Jojo, a man of immense corpulence. Valadon and Mousis, so Jourdain was told, went there regularly when staying in the nearby rue Cortot. It was not yet, he noted, the meeting place of genius.

"À rentrait, par la ru' des Saules ru' Saint-Vincent," sang Bruant, and in 1900 he bought the Lapin Agile. His own home was up in the rue Cortot. There was a flat piece of ground in front of the house, and here Bruant had a miniature bicycle track built. Every morning he pedalled round and round, "to air his lungs," as he put it. He was a rich man now, so he could live as he liked and dress as the fancy took him. He wore sabots, wide country trousers and an officer's kepi on his head. He kept chickens in his garden and had a dozen dogs. He lounged about in the sunshine, but his business acumen had not deserted him.

Under his aegis the Lapin Agile became the center of Montmartre life. He had been lucky enough to meet Frédéric Gérard, known to everyone as Frédé, and he was clever enough to put him into the Lapin as manager. At first, Frédé wore a moustache; but then, after the Lapin had become famous, his venerable beard grew.

Bruant left the running of the Lapin entirely to Frédé. When he went down to the cabaret he considered himself one of the guests, but woe to the underlings if they addressed him as Monsieur instead of Chansonnier Populaire as he insisted. The artists and writers called him Grand-père whether he liked it or not. His ballads were sung every night, of course. Frédé himself sang mostly seventeenth-century French songs, accompanying himself on the guitar. He thought more of painters than of writers. "You only have to do nothing to become famous," he would say.

The young writers and poets flocked to him: among them Pierre Mac Orlan, André Warnod, Guillaume Apollinaire and Max Jacob, who belonged to the group of painters too. The painters included Picasso, Girieud, Lombard, Gassier, Picard-Ledour, Falké, Verdilham, Zig Brunner, Maclet and Poulbot. Picasso usually sat facing his painting *The Harlequin*, wearing overalls. Max Jacob wore a frock coat and top hat, as his brother was a tailor and extended him credit. Now and then Apollinaire was accompanied by Marie Laurencin who, wrote Warnod, brought to the Lapin the elegance and refinement of a well-brought-up young lady.

They were gloriously poor. To be "gloriously poor" was surely a phrase coined by those who suffer from dyspepsia because they never have less than five courses at a meal; or perhaps it originated with profound thinkers who admire the penniless because they have no responsibility or worries? How to pay for the next slice of bread and bit of sausage seems from the distance no worry at all. The gloriously poor in the Lapin Agile worried about the next bottle of wine. The more refined, like Max Jacob, worried about the next bottle of ether, though it cost only thirty centimes in the pharmacy. The more expensive hashish would come in with Modigliani.

One was so gloriously poor that when Max Jacob went to dine in the rue Gros with Guillaume Apollinaire they had to borrow Max Jacob's fare back to the Butte from the concierge. When Gaston de Pawlowski, editor in chief of *Comedia*, called on Bottini, the painter, Bottini heated the teapot on the gas lamp just under his window. Vlaminck walked the whole way to the Butte when visiting friends because he could not afford to use public transport.

Still, there were ways and means of earning a few sous. Van Dongen for instance sold newspapers. Once André Warnod and René Denèfle were called in by the wife of a paralyzed old painter who wanted to sell all her husband's paintings—a final sale as there were no more to come. However, the dealer thought there were not enough of them to make it worth his while. The two young men added several pictures to the collection which they had painted in the husband's style. The satisfied dealer bought the lot.

One drank heavily in the Lapin Agile. Drink, friendship and hope—all three exaggerated—were the essence of life. Poetry was recited, songs were sung, from Bruant and Borel to Gaston Couté, from *Roi, fais battre le tambour* to *Le temps des cerises*. On his first night in the Lapin, Carco stood on a table and practically committed sacrilege by imitating the singers of the Concert Mayol. Low, popular songs were barred from the Lapin as the intellectual clientele abhorred café-concert couplets, but when he mimed the fashionable singer of *Mains de femmes* they saw that he was one of them, a real poet. Frédé offered him a drink, which was akin to an accolade. Carco was so delighted that he immediately threw up his job with the Paris Water Board and joined the group. As he could not afford to fend for himself he went to stay with his friend Édouard Gazanion, which was in the best Montmartre tradition. Everybody lived with his neighbour.

To enter into this world one needed qualifications, none of which Utrillo possessed. He was shy and frightened of crowds, bad at repartee and he had no liking for elaborate practical jokes in which the habitués of the Lapin much enjoyed. Their most famous practical joke concerned a donkey, and casts a strong light on the world which was to surround Utrillo after his return to the Butte.

Frédé's mother was a midwife and resided in the suburbs. She owned a stubborn donkey called Lolo. When the midwife rode into Paris, Lolo saw to it that they arrived disgracefully late.

Lolo inspired Roland Dorgelès with a capital idea. Dorgelès had a poor opinion of the futurists, and taking Warnod into his confidence he issued a manifesto in the style of Marinetti, suggesting among other constructive ideas that all masterpieces should be burnt. The manifesto was signed "Boronali," an anagram of Aliboron. ("Aliboron" means a "conceited ass," and comes from La Fontaine's fable *Les voleurs et l'âne*.) Boronali sounded perfectly Italian, and a futurist painter should have an Italian name. A few newspapers printed the manifesto, their editors taking Boronali for a dissident futurist.

Dorgelès and Warnod asked Frédé to lend them Lolo. First Frédé refused, probably because he already had enough painters around him without needing Lolo to swell their number. Eventually he gave in. The conspirators had one fear: Would the world believe that Lolo was Boronali, that is, that Lolo had executed a futurist painting? They considered asking the police to witness Lolo at work. However, on second thought, they decided against it. Dorgelès went instead to a *huissier*, a bailiff, but first bought himself a rosette of the Legion of Honour in order to impress him. M. Brionne, the bailiff, turned out to be young and helpful, and he agreed to be officially present when Lolo painted the picture.

"My friend Joachim-Raphaël Boronali," said Dorgelès, introducing Lolo to him.

M. Brionne did not offer his hand but gave Lolo a cigarette, which the donkey chewed contentedly. Lolo had on one occasion eaten Picasso's pipe tobacco, and was a regular brandy drinker. A paintbrush dipped in ultramarine was tied to Lolo's tail, an easel with a blank canvas was set up behind the donkey, and after a few seconds of breathless waiting the donkey's tail began to move, each movement leaving a patch of paint on the canvas. When they thought there was enough ultramarine on the canvas Warnod and Dorgelès replaced the brush with one dipped in red. Whenever Lolo seemed to tire of the effort a carrot was produced to induce fresh energy. "You can see the donkey is painting all alone," Dorgelès said. M. Brionne assured him that he had written it down.

"You two are stupider than the donkey," said Berthe, the waitress, coming on the scene.

Lolo grew tired, so Frédé was called in, and he sang *Le temps des cerises*, Lolo's favourite tune, into the donkey's ear. The painting was finished with verve and aplomb. The title was quickly found: *The Sun Sets over the Adriatic*.

The picture was shown at the Salon des Indépendants. There was no scandal; in fact some visitors to the exhibition definitely praised it. "I like it," a short woman observed; "it is so individual." Others said, "But this is by Boronali, the one who published the manifesto." A lady turned to her husband: "Where is the sea?" He pointed at the background. "But it is all red," she exclaimed. Her husband calmed her, saying a red sea was in the best futurist tradition.

When the joke had lasted long enough the conspirators decided to reveal the truth. Dorgelès forced his way into the office of the editor in chief of *Le Matin*. "Your art critic," he said severely, "has written offensively of my friend Joachim-Raphaël Boronali. Read this document, and, I am sure, your attitude will change."

He gave the editor M. Brionne's official statement. The editor was stunned, but soon his professional flair got the better of him, and Dorgelès agreed to the story being published exclusively in *Le Matin*. It appeared under the heading: *A Donkey Head of a Movement*.

The Lapin Agile profited from the joke, and so did Lolo, for on page 682 of Bénézit's *Dictionnaire des Peintres* it found immortality between Bonnard and Bottini: "Boronali, J-R., painter born in Genoa in the XIX century (Italian school)."

In its old age Lolo was taken to Saint-Cyr-sur-Morin, so that its eventful life might end quietly in the country. This was not to be. Lolo slipped into the river off an embankment and was drowned. Dorgelès was convinced that it was no accident. In his opinion Boronali had committed suicide in desperate longing for the Butte-Montmartre.

1

VALADON and Mousis rented the ground-floor flat at 12 rue Cortot. The house had been built in the seventh century, and one of its first owners was Claude Roze, Sieur de Rosimond, usually called Roze de Rosimond, as he acted under that name. He appeared in the theater of the Hôtel de Bourgogne, where he took the same parts as Molière, and, like Molière, he died while playing in *Le malade imaginaire*. Émile Bernard, the painter, a friend of Cézanne and editor of *La Rénovation Esthétique*, lived above Valadon. "No one shall enter here who does not believe in God, Raphael and Titian," was written over his door.

When Utrillo arrived in the rue Cortot his mother gave him all the liberty he wanted. She was sure she could trust him. Valadon knew from her own experience that painting kept her on an unwavering path, her destination perfection. Her son was dedicated to his painting, therefore, his path would be similar to hers. She saw no cause to worry.

The Butte had changed since his childhood and schooldays. The Sacré-Coeur was free of scaffolding, new houses were rising and he saw fresh faces everywhere. Yet, the Maquis was still there with its huts, peopled by tramps and *rapins* (art students) with their girls, usually middle-class girls, who had run away from home to sample the gay life of the Butte. There was drink and sex all round him; bistros abounded. Utrillo set up his easel at some street corner and painted.

He drew with a soft pencil, then put on a thick layer of colour, and began to paint when the canvas, or generally the cardboard, was half dry. He started at the bottom of the cardboard or canvas, working his way up. (Corot had painted likewise.) Instinctively, without even bothering to ask himself or anyone else the reason, he became a landscape painter, a painter of streets and houses and the trees that went with streets and houses. In all his life he painted only one portrait, that of a Japanese who, unable to find the street he was looking for on the Butte, asked Utrillo to direct him. Because Utrillo painted mostly the streets of Montmartre he entered the family of Montmartre painters.

Georges Michel (no forbear of Michel Georges-Michel, the writer), born in Paris in 1763, had been the father of the Montmartre painters. He ran away at the age of 15 with Marguerite Legros, a washerwoman, was a father at 16, and had five children by the time he was 20. In 1783 a colonel took him to Normandy with his regiment. He was given food and lodging in return for the drawings he made. When he was given the rank of lieutenant, he was able to send money to his family in Paris. There is no trace of him during the Revolution; all one knows is that he came back from Switzerland when things had quieted down. He struck up a friendship with Bruandet, the painter and crook who had killed his unfaithful sweetheart by throwing her through a window. Bruandet vanished into the Forest of Fontainebleau, where he spent his time painting trees.

Michel aspired to a less exciting life. He frequented the home of Mme. Vigée-Lebrun, who was then 50.

Michel painted Montmartre landscapes; he was known as the Ruysdael of Montmartre, but his mills and vineyards had no financial success. He painted Belleville too, all in rich colours with a strong feeling of happiness. He could walk with his wife for hours on the Butte, and they were often seen coming home to Paris after nightfall.

Though he had been kept for years by the colonel, who had been a member of the *ancien régime*, no one could mention it in his presence without incurring his wrath. He had a long body, short legs, black hair and eyes. He believed in the Supreme Being, but on his deathbed in 1834 he made his peace with God. He was practically forgotten after his death.

"A poor devil of a French landscape painter," Sainte-Beuve wrote of him, "who had a feeling for and love of simple things."

Now forty-eight of his drawings bound in two albums are in the Louvre. His water colours were perhaps the best of his work.

Jean-Louis-André-Théodore Géricault was considered by the Montmartrois a Montmartrois painter, that is, a member of the same family of painters as Utrillo, on account of his painting *Four de Plâtre* depicting a Montmartre kiln, which now hangs in the Louvre.

Camille Corot painted the Moulin de la Galette in 1840, also the rue Saint-Vincent; Antoine Vollon the Moulin de la Galette in 1860; Napoléon-Joseph Bellardel the rue d'Orchampt in 1864; and Louis Daguerre, who was influenced by Bonington, painted panoramas of Paris in the 1840s from the mills of Montmartre. One can add to the list Théodore Rousseau, Van Gogh and Renoir, though one cannot call any of them a Montmartre painter in the sense that Georges Michel had been. His true successor was Johan Barthold Jongkind, who lived in Montmartre in the 1850s, first in the Place Pigalle, then near the Place Blanche. He loved Montmartre like Michel before him and Utrillo after him. It was love that bound their art to the hillock. He was an admirable water colourist and sketcher, a painter of exceptional talent, forerunner of realism and impressionism, finding his lonely niche somewhere between the two.

If Jongkind was the heir to Georges Michel then Utrillo was the heir to Jongkind, though it is almost certain that Utrillo never took the trouble to look at his pictures. He had no curiosity about what other painters did or had done. He knew only his mother's paintings, nobody else's. "My mother let me paint as I liked. She is too great an artist to interfere with another artist even if he is her son." True, there was the influence of Pissarro and Sisley, but he already had finished with that—or so he believed. When chatting with Coquiot, who often talked with Utrillo and Valadon, he denied that he had been influenced by Pissarro. Perhaps there was some similarity in his earlier work but that was all.

The year 1903, Utrillo explained to Coquiot, was the period of Pierrefitte-Montmagny, also of the quays of the Seine in Paris. "I always painted with my mother." Whenever mother and son went painting together they did not paint side by side but Valadon took up a position in front of him. He painted direct from nature. Now and then, he admitted, he played truant. As he progressed in his art he found that his paintings were becoming too sleek, too glossy. He could give no reason for that. Later he wanted to paint in black and white; however his walls were not white enough and his trees never black enough. That gave him the idea that plaster alone could give the white he needed. So he began to use plaster in his painting, mixing white zinc with it. He obtained the plaster straight from walls, scratching off small bits of it which, mixed with the zinc, gave his walls their natural colour.

When Valadon saw the first painting in which he had used plaster, she asked him how he had achieved the effect. "With plaster," he said.

"You are mad," she said. "It won't hold."

Amazingly, the paintings in which he used plaster weathered better than much of his other work. The colours remained the same, quite miraculously, most painters would think. There was something else miraculous in Utrillo's art: on the one hand he relied completely on instinct, on the other on power of observation. He had the eye of an architect and the heart of a sad, though deeply lyrical, poet. When at his best, eye and heart worked in unison.

"I give my instinct free rein," he said. "Some of my paintings are like bas-reliefs because I come back several times on my colours. My skies alone are arranged so that they should be as limpid and transparent as possible."

He put his colours on strongly. He raised walls, telling himself he was the mason, the carpenter, the tiler, though he went for the details only when all was in place, including the top and bottom colours. The walls then had to be punctured with windows, the roofs covered with slates or tiles, then came the shutters. He always counted the windows. "You have no idea how necessary details are," he explained. Details fascinated him. The first thing he asked anyone he met was his height.

His streets were lonely streets. One finds it amazing that so young a man, who himself shunned the company of his fellows, could express on cardboard or canvas the sense of loneliness and isolation streets can inspire. His houses are not the homes of gay families playing one parlour game after the other. They are empty houses: nobody lives in them. Though Valadon used to say that exciting things happen behind Utrillo's windows, one has the feeling that nothing takes place behind them, and if, by chance, there are inhabitants, they neither cook nor copulate. In his paintings of Montmagny one feels the desolation of suburban life. The walls are waiting for rain, the cobbles for nobody, and the distant church spire seems the only hope left. Large signs on the walls proclaim in vain that coal, wood and wine can be purchased. One knows instinctively that shops and taverns have sold out long ago.

Valadon forced Utrillo to destroy the paintings she found bad. It was due to her judgement and her eye for good painting that one finds his early work free of the faults and errors of the beginner. He succeeded, thanks to her. Without her continuous scolding, explaining and encouraging he might have taken the wrong road. In every creative person there lives a third-rate creature who bursts to have his say. Valadon destroyed the third-rate creature in Utrillo the artist. It was a different matter with Utrillo the man.

2

One day Utrillo went down to the Seine to paint the quays. In those days taverns abounded on the quays. Whether he fell in with bargemen and similar heavy drinkers or could not resist the call of the taverns is of no real importance: the fact is that he returned to the rue Cortot completely drunk, hardly able to keep on his feet. "Is that you, Maurice?" Valadon called from the next room. He was so drunk that he could not answer. She came in and made him lie down on the sofa. "Maurice, my little one, I don't want you to go mad," she cried, petrified. It took her some time to grasp that he was paralyzed with drink. The realization gave her, as she said afterward, one of the worst shocks of her life: painting had not cured her son. Because she seldom touched a glass and was generally abstinent, she could not imagine anyone capable of getting into such a state and still pursuing an artist's career. Yet, Utrillo rose in the morning as though nothing had happened and went painting.

"You are more annoyed with him when he gets his perspective wrong than when he comes home drunk," Mousis is reputed to have said to her.

To understand Valadon's attitude toward her son's drinking, one should not forget that she knew little of the ways of the world. She was uneducated, and little interested her outside her overriding passion for painting. Except for Mousis, who always let her have her way, the men she came in contact with were artists, that is, men who were not bound by convention and who followed no rules other than their inspiration. Most of them were heavy drinkers, therefore, she never was as dismayed by her son's drinking as would have been a mother who led a humdrum conventional life. The expression "one's place in society" had no significance for her. So all she worried about was whether drink interfered with her son's talent. Apparently it did not. Of course, she feared that drinking might undermine his health. However, it did not seem to do so. Now and then she thought that drink might drive him mad, but such thoughts were more like nightmares than facts about which something should be done. She was a complete tyro in medical matters. Since she only read books on art, she had little idea of the misery and unhappiness drunkenness can cause socially and individually, as depicted in so many novels and tracts of her time. That drink was not her son's only trouble she refused to contemplate, or perhaps, to put it more simply, she was, owing to her lack of education and limited interests, unable to see it. Yet the other was as weighty a calamity as his drinking.

Utrillo had the unfortunate knack of irritating and annoying people even when he did not drink. It was his bad luck to be the target of all who were malicious, all who had sadistic leanings, and all who enjoyed giving pain to their neighbours. It had been the same when he was a schoolboy.

An old resident of the Butte who remembered Utrillo's return from Montmagny in 1903 described this constant persecution. "His mother dressed him well," he said. "He wore a well-cut black suit made of excellent cloth. He was better dressed than most people on the Butte, so they couldn't have taken him for a tramp. He was usually sober when he went painting, and he took no notice of other people while he worked, yet somehow he drew them like a magnet. There are poor dogs which are such magnets. All other dogs fall on them, though they are inoffensive. With Maurice it always began with children. Other painters they left unmolested, but they came and laughed at Utrillo. Then Maurice would become excited and roll his eyes. He always rolled his eyes when he was overexcited. The children backed away, jeering. Then the grownups stepped in. By then Maurice was waving his arms. He swore at them. They upset his easel, trampled on his canvas. Often there were fights. Poor Maurice was always the loser." The old resident shook his head. "He was like those poor dogs."

After the fights Utrillo usually rushed into the nearest bistro and swallowed large quantities of wine. With the wine inside him he became an even more pathetic figure, and, as though the drink had set some engine turning at full speed inside him, he ran like a man pursued, from one bistro to another. The passers-by jeered, and he shrieked and shouted insults. If he was thrown out of one bistro he ran into the next, where he started rampaging and breaking things. Francis Carco, the excellent novelist and shrewd chronicler of bohemian life, considered the Butte Utrillo's daily Calvary, the bistros the stations of his Cross.

It was a vicious circle. The more enemies he had, the drunker he got. The drunker he got, the more enemies he made. Yet he did not drink because of them: they only exaggerated his behaviour. He could drink himself to oblivion behind locked doors.

The young man drank like an old tramp. He had no flashes of gaiety; the bistros did not ring with his laughter; and if he laughed he laughed like a village idiot. Companionship meant nothing to him when he was in his cups. He preferred to be alone with the wine. He sought in drink not what so many seek—to expand, to feel the pulse of life beat faster and not care a damn about the hangover to come—but oblivion, the total empty darkness of death. He had a strong constitution, so it took him many hours to satisfy his death wish.

He had no pride and no sense of shame when drunk. There lives a suppressed buffoon in most of us: Utrillo gave full rein to the buffoon in him. Frequently the buffoon turned into a sad, sobbing clown. "Utrillo was the most beaten-up man of his time," said his friend Edmond Heuzé, the painter.

"I saw Maurice lying one dawn in the snow in the rue Lepic," an old street-corner painter said of him. "He looked really beautiful in his black suit in the white snow. He lay on his belly, a cigarette end stuck to his lower lip. He never moved. He was kicked by a few passers-by, but eventually we dragged him home to his mother."

His mother put him to bed, scolded him when he awoke, and Utrillo cried bitterly, promising to mend his ways. Valadon had not given up hope. He was painting, therefore, all would be well yet. Recognition would come to him one day, and then he would surely stop making a public fool of himself. Famous painters respect the world, since it is the world that provides them with their fame. With recognition, thought Valadon, he would become a new man. She concentrated on teaching and encouraging the painter while she tried to keep the man in check.

There was for the moment, Valadon believed, one practical solution: deny him money. Valadon could not have foreseen the deplorable consequences of withholding his pocket money. Utrillo's answer was to sell his paintings for wine—one painting, one litre! Every bistro keeper in Montmartre dreams of discovering another Utrillo: those paintings exchanged for a litre of wine are now worth a king's ransom.

Some landlords cheated him. " 'Finish your masterpiece,' one of them said to me," Utrillo complained, "but when the masterpiece was finished he paid for only one round."

Utrillo's paintings pleased the ordinary folk; otherwise he could not have obtained the wine. The landlords kept the paintings because they enjoyed looking at them, and some were reluctant to sell even when their profit would have been handsome. The customers liked the paintings too. Yet neither landlords

nor customers could stomach Utrillo himself. Here one is forced
to take notice of the gulf between Utrillo the man and Utrillo
the painter. It is a gulf that no theory could bridge. Which
of the two was the real Utrillo? Evidently both. Utrillo the
man went on suffering from the contempt of his fellow man,
while Utrillo the painter could command a litre of wine or
even a few sous for a painting.

Every possible humiliation was thought up by his enemies.
They would sit on a chair near the bistro door, waiting for
drunken Maumau, as many called him. Then, on his way out,
they would lift a leg to trip him. When he fell flat on his face
they laughed delightedly. His wine was mixed with eau de
Cologne or paraffin oil when he was not looking. Yet, he drained
the glass without flinching. At the next drink cigar or cigarette
ash was knocked into his glass. Utrillo tossed the ash down
with the wine.

In the 1950s a little wizened, regularly unemployed musician
used to boast in the bistros to anybody who was willing to
listen of having made water into Utrillo's glass while he was
out at the lavatory. "It was a large enough glass to hold a pint,"
he explained to his admiring audience. "Of course, I mixed it
with plenty of wine." The man shook with laughter. "Now he
is rich and an officer of the Legion of Honour, yet he drank
my urine."

Not only cruel men molested Utrillo. In the rue de Caulaincourt a quiet, inoffensive garage keeper, potbellied and grey-
haired, gave Utrillo a beating when both of them were already
in their forties.

"He came into my garage," the man said. "He was drunk.
He stood there swaying, foaming at the mouth and gesticulating wildly. I told him to get out. He pretended not to understand me. I gave him a good beating, then kicked his backside.
You ought to have seen him running away."

"But why did you want to beat him?" the garage keeper was

asked. "He was probably too drunk to understand you. Anyway, he did you no harm."

"He made me see red."

"Did you know who he was?"

"Of course I did. I am not afraid of any Monsieur Utrillo. Besides, I'd given him a previous beating. That was when we were both young."

"What was the reason that time?"

"He made me see red. I won't have chaps like him trying to be funny with me. I hit first."

There it was in a nutshell. Utrillo gave the impression that he wanted to attack. Yet not even his oldest enemies could recall a single instance when Utrillo caused anyone bodily harm. However much they would have liked to, not one of them could give a single example. None the less they were convinced that they had hit Utrillo in self-defense.

But why should dozens and dozens have thought that Utrillo wanted to attack them? The usual answer was that he made threatening gestures, ground his teeth, and had an evil expression. The evil expression, like the threatening gestures, was merely the kind of attitude found in children who suddenly become aggressive and bad-tempered. The doctors themselves said that Utrillo had a childlike nature—in brief, he had never matured.

Children do not like policemen, so Utrillo fell out with the police. Tavern keepers sent for them whenever he became obstreperous. To be thrown out meant going without drink, therefore, he clung to tables, counter or curtain, anything which kept him near the bottle. The police came and in his panic, he resisted them, trying to bite them like a frightened animal. One is constantly reminded of the poor dog which all other dogs attack. He received a severe beating and was taken to the police station, where a more violent beating, called *passer à tabac*, followed. The police came to know him well; in fact, policemen used to wait for him at night when they had nothing better to do.

Even when he left a bistro peacefully the police were there to receive him. They pounced on him, and, kicking and biting, he tried to resist arrest. The policemen pushed him into a cell and gave him his regular thrashing. In the morning he emerged in a pitiable state, covered in filth, his trousers torn; he wandered about the streets afraid to go home. But he slunk home in the end, and, though still shaken, took brush and palette and started to paint.

Yet there were exceptions, because above all his faults and failings he was a guileless, fundamentally kind man. "I liked him," said a bistro keeper to Carco. "He was so honest. If you knew how to take him he never said no to you."

He gave two sous to an old charwoman of the Butte because she had dropped the bottle of wine she was carrying. He felt truly sorry for her, and apologized for having only two sous on him.

Now and then when he lay drunk in the gutter Utrillo shrieked that he was the devil. He was often seen holding an empty bottle in his arms, fondling it as a loving mother fondles a baby. He was timid when he did not feel persecuted. If one spoke to him he did not answer. On the other hand, he would mutter to himself, repeating the same word twenty times. In the Lapin Agile he had his own corner. The noisy, witty crowd was not for him. He sat alone, drinking quietly, looking at nobody. He was often hungry because he had not dared go home. Then Berthe, the waitress, gave him a slice of bread and butter in the kitchen. If he had a fight in the Lapin it was with an outsider. The crowd let him be, though they did not take to him. He lived through the golden age of Montmartre practically unconscious of it. He was in it but not of it. None the less, if one speaks of the Lapin, Utrillo leaps to mind as quickly as Max Jacob, Picasso or Apollinaire.

"Litrillo, Litrillo," chanted the children when he set up his easel at the corner.

He had been nicknamed Litrillo because of the litres of wine he drank.

"Maumau, Maumau," shrieked the old women, looking out of their windows.

"Good morning, painter," said the passers-by with heavy sarcasm.

Workmen and their families were especially vile to him. They were convinced that he was stark raving mad. They shouted that he should be locked up, though not one of them could know that he had been in Sainte-Anne. In his own defense poor Litrillo coined his famous phrase: "I am not mad: I am an alcoholic."

The fear of being taken for a madman haunted him ever since the day his mother took him for the first time to Sainte-Anne. Although the word mad was used innocently—you are mad if you marry young, you are mad if you give away money, you are mad if you quarrel with your boss and so on—it always had a sinister ring for Utrillo. It reminded him of Sainte-Anne, the panic he felt there and the fear he saw in his mother's eyes. It was not a word to trifle with, for it had a definite meaning, namely a lunatic asylum, where you were watched, controlled, isolated from your mother and unable to drink.

3

Alphonse Quizet was born in the year 1885 at 44 Quai de l'Hôtel de Ville, a noisy neighbourhood with little shops and taverns, peopled by carters with their huge, caparisoned Percheron horses, and shouting bargemen. He was one of six children. Number 44 was a bistro-restaurant, Papa Quizet the owner. The father was a humourless man who had come from Saint-Flour like many other Auvergnats to sell water at one sou a large bucketful. He prospered as a water carrier and bought the bistro-restaurant. He was also a sergeant in the Municipal Guard.

Little Alphonse went to school in the rue François-Miron, where the schoolmistress sucked pills of potassium chlorate which gave her breath a sickly smell. Quizet gave the school a wide berth. It took the family quite a while to apprehend that he was playing truant. His next school was run by nuns, but he preferred the company of Percherons and tramps. The day came when he was taken bleeding to the pharmacy. The Louvre-Charenton tram had run over him but without the wheels touching him.

When he was eight years old Papa Quizet moved his family to Pigalle, where he had bought a hotel. Quizet now attended a school in the rue Lepic. He and his schoolmates decided to explore the heights of Montmartre. They found themselves near the Lapin Agile, still the Cabaret des Assassins in those days. They peeped in and saw a horrible painting of a man murdering an entire family (Tropmann). There Quizet understood, as he said years later, the strength of pictorial art. The shuddering boys climbed up to the Place du Tertre. There he realized the true meaning of the Butte. However, he didn't decide to become a painter till after his first visit to the Louvre. He took to water colours, painting in his spare time. He had met an old water-colourist from whom he sought advice.

"With water colours," the old man said, "as their name implies, use water, plenty of water and very little colour."

When he grew up he found employment as a draughtsman with the Compagnie des Autobus, and in spite of the considerable success of his painting he remained with the company until the age of retirement.

On a sunny morning in 1905 Quizet went painting in the rue Cortot. He set up his easel at the top of the street and a curious, rather haggard young man stopped beside him.

"What sort of painting is that?" the young man asked.

"Water-colour painting," Quizet replied.

"How does one paint with water colours?"

Quizet quoted the old water-colourist.

"I'd like to try myself," the young man said, "but people interfere with me and—

"And what else?"

"I have no money to buy myself paints."

A woman appeared at a window, holding a palette. "Maurice," she called, "go and fetch the bread. Run."

"That's my mother." Utrillo explained. "She's a painter."

"In that case," said Quizet, "steal some of her paints."

Utrillo had lied to him. The last thing Valadon would have done was keep him from painting. To make him work was her one hope for his salvation. She gave him as many tubes as he needed. Utrillo had lied because lying had become with him a form of self-defense. He might even have hoped that Quizet would give him the money to buy paints, which he could then have spent on drink.

Utrillo and Quizet became good friends. As they painted together, their intimacy grew, yet Utrillo, who loved his mother with all his heart, never confessed to Quizet that he had lied about her. He never retracted his own lies or corrected anybody else's. When he read the worst falsehoods about himself he shrugged his shoulders and left it at that. He stuck to his own lies because he told them only to suit himself. Truth expressed in words had no importance for him, but in his paintings, it was supreme.

Although Quizet and Utrillo admired each other's work, discussed painting, and set up their easels side by side, they had no influence on each other. If one looks at a good Utrillo, one feels the fervour of his extraordinary talent; when one looks at Quizet's work, one is charmed. Quizet could sit in an office for six days a week until the age of retirement. The job Utrillo held the longest had lasted for less than a month. Streets for Quizet meant going from one place to the other. He reproduced them with enchanting serenity—one could linger there. But not in Utrillo's, for whom streets meant torment and loneliness. However, the basic difference between the two was that the hand that held Utrillo's brush was incomparably the more talented.

"If you lived in a house full of Utrillos," said an admirer of Quizet, "you would leave the house after a month because of their stifling sense of drama. Whereas with Quizets you would almost forget that you had any paintings at all."

Painting with a friend was very much in the fashion. Quizet often went painting with another young man, André Utter, a native of Montmartre like Utrillo. Utter was of Hanseatic origin. His forebears had been shipwrights who had settled in Kehl on the Rhine in the last century. Utter's father followed the same trade, but the sheathing of vessels with metal came to an end, so he emigrated to Paris, where he earned his living as a plumber. The family lived in the rue de Clignancourt, and on March 28, 1886, André Utter was born in a narrow, dark room behind his father's workshop. He had two sisters, no brothers, and so his father expected him to follow in his footsteps. However, the son preferred to starve on the Butte, usually in the Lapin Agile, rather than become a plumber. The friend of Heuzé and Quizet, with his rosy cheeks and wavy fair hair, wanted to be a painter. His parents took a poor view of that, but Utter persevered.

He had a fine gift for friendship and comradeship and was much liked in the Lapin Agile, where one often saw him in his plumber's overalls, for his father still forced him to work for him. Later he was employed by the electricity board in the Avenue Trudaine. He radiated, as the Montmartrois put it, electricity to his beloved Butte. Shortly afterward he left his parents for good.

Utter was a handsome young man with a strong personality. He enjoyed talking about himself. He had no false modesty and he could invent episodes with the same ease as Valadon or Utrillo; none the less one never heard him talk of his parents. The parting of ways, one feels, had not been a moving family scene with parents and sisters waving tear-sodden handkerchiefs as the dear one left to make his way in the world.

The spirit of Montmartre, on the other hand, certainly cared for him. Utter embodied many of the characteristics of a fine, strapping man beloved of Montmartre. He could drink like a fish, yet he knew how to hold his liquor; he could sing and shout as loudly as anyone, yet he did not get mixed up in brawls; and he had an extravagant sense of his own importance as a Montmartrois. "Montmartre means drink and scandal," was his description of his spiritual and temporal home. In spite of his exaggerated personality he had his feet firmly planted on the ground. He had a strong commercial sense and understood the meaning of money. The plumber's son craved for luxury; he loved showing off. He was still under twenty when, on one of their excursions, he and Edmond Heuzé chose to paint the rue Cortot. They worked away, concentrating with all their young energies, when they suddenly caught sight of a short, thin woman bearing down on them. She had two enormous dogs on a lead. Her eyes were astonishingly light, her hair black and parted down the middle, her gait rhythmical. She was Suzanne Valadon.

She stopped to look at their work. "One doesn't paint the sky as one paints the ground," she said cryptically, and then moved on. The two young men stared after her.

Utter was a good painter though not a great painter. If his life had not been sandwiched between the lives of Valadon and Utrillo, his work would have been more esteemed. He had a thorough knowledge of painting. One was fascinated when he spoke of the technical problems of drawing and painting. He was a good listener too. If one spoke of a subject he was un-acquainted with he listened not only politely but also intently.

He became slightly ridiculous when he played the great gentleman. He was a vain man, exceedingly proud of his calves and
ankles.

In 1908 Utter went to Pierrefitte-Montmagny for a brief
rest. He did not enjoy his stay there. It was one thing to paint
landscapes; quite another to live in one of them. In the course
of a solitary walk late at night he saw another young man, tall
and dark and not too steady on his feet. The young man was
muttering to himself: "Montmartre . . . disgusting bistro."
It was Utrillo. Utter agreed to help him home and thus he met
the woman with the light eyes again. He was impressed by her
and the fact that both mother and son were painters. In
those days he had not made his final choice, he was still at
loggerheads with his parents, so meeting two painters did a lot
of good for his morale. It is good for the soul to feel one is
not alone on the self-appointed road. He returned to Paris more
sure of himself.

Utter and Valadon did not meet again for a long time. The
story has it that once, while repairing some pipes in the courtyard of 12 rue Cortot, Valadon was at the window and when
she saw him she called him in.

"If I wanted a man," she declared to Pedro Creixams, the
Spanish-Catalan painter who lived on the Butte and was a
tenacious though gentle lady-killer in whom women liked to
confide, "I made no bones about it. I was usually the one who
undressed first."

She and Utter became lovers.

"Of all my men I loved André best," Valadon said in old age,
"because he made me suffer most."

She asked Utter frequently to Montmagny. Mousis could not
help noticing the state of affairs. The lovers were too intense to
be able to keep him in blissful ignorance.

"Mousis told my mother to choose between him and her
drunken son," Utrillo liked to relate. "She chose me."

That was flattering but it was not the truth. Mousis left because of Utter and all Valadon wanted was to remain undisturbed with her lover. Mousis was a nuisance, Mousis must go. So Mousis went. The shadowy businessman vanished into the shadows, and Valadon, Utrillo and Utter hardly ever spoke of him again. "I don't remember him," was Valadon's reply to a friend who wished to find out what had become of Mousis. This of the man who had footed the bills of mother and son. For sixteen years, they had not gone short of anything.

Utrillo was three years older than Utter and the relationship between them was bound to be awkward. Before Utrillo became successful, Utter did not have a high opinion of his painting. "His childish painting left us indifferent," Utter said to Heuzé. "We all painted like that at our elementary schools."

On the other hand, Utrillo owed him a great deal. Nobody is born an expert—much of art has to be learnt. It was Utter who taught Utrillo how to put one colour on the other. Utter might have been a mediocre painter yet he was an expert in teaching. Valadon was too brilliant a painter to look at the humdrum and the prosaic: Utter looked at it methodically.

Mousis' departure brought about the end of Montmagny and of Valadon's first period in the rue Cortot. She found a flat at 5 Impasse Guelma, yet went on visiting 12 rue Cortot as Degas had his studio on the second floor. Degas gave her permission to sleep in the studio whenever she wanted. She took advantage of the offer and spent many nights there, probably because she did not want to bring Utter home since her mother still lived with her. Valadon and Utter conducted their love life in Degas' studio.

Degas lived in Passy and was never in the rue Cortot in the evenings; there was, therefore, no cause to fear that he would find them. Early one morning, however, Degas went to his window in Passy and saw the aurora borealis over Paris and it fascinated him so much that he wanted to paint it immediately. He took a cab to his studio. When the lovers heard Degas mounting the twisting, dangerous stairs, Valadon hid Utter in the large wardrobe in the studio.

Degas sensed something strange, looked here, looked there, eventually opened the wardrobe and saw Utter standing in it stark naked.

"What are you doing here, young man?" Degas shouted.

"Waiting for a tram," said Utter.

Degas ordered them out of the studio and refused to see his terrible Maria again.

——— *The Road to Fame*

1

*U*TRILLO was called up for military service. He hastened to Clignancourt to present himself before the medical board, for he loved uniforms, military bands and all the paraphernalia of a soldier's life. And, as his paintings show, he especially loved flags. "Flags flutter: houses stay put," he observed. "That was one of the first things I learnt."

It was a sad scene at Clignancourt. As the undernourished proletarian young men filed past the board, the army doctors called out their physical shortcomings: tuberculosis, rickets, rheumatic fever. When Utrillo appeared the colonel said, "At last a robust fellow," and shook him by the hand. Utrillo was delighted. He now had proof that he was a normal, fine fellow, better developed than most young men of his age.

He went to celebrate it with huge libations. In barracks he would be away from maternal supervision, he would wear a uniform and could spend his free time in the bistros unmolested

by his enemies. It did not enter his head that he might make
fresh enemies among his comrades-at-arms. But Valadon saw
Drs. Ettlinger and Vallon, from whom she obtained certificates
which she sent to the medical board: the robust fellow was
turned down. Utrillo was heartbroken. Still, he would have
plenty of liberty at home.

The arrival of Utter in Valadon's life had made it possible
for Utrillo to go his own way. Her early years with Utter were
lived with such intensity that she had little time left to exercise
control over her son. Moreover, one can't enjoy a love affair
in the continual presence of a rowdy third party. Twenty-six
years old, Utrillo left, though the umbilical cord was not sev-
ered.

He first found lodgings at 2 rue Cortot in an old house that
has since been pulled down. Then he tried some of the squalid
hotels in the neighbourhood. He had to leave each one for the
same reason—not even the lowest inn would tolerate his rampaging. Then his luck changed: he fell in with Gay, a retired
police sergeant, whom everyone called *Père* Gay. He was the
proud owner of a bistro, Le Casse-Croûte, and lived above it
with his wife. They had a few spare rooms and on Valadon's
insistence they accepted Utrillo as a lodger. There was no need
to point out to Gay who the new lodger was. The Casse-Croûte
was in the rue Paul-Féval, not far from the rue Saint-Vincent
and the rue Cortot, so Gay knew all about Litrillo and his
doings. The retired police sergeant had a liking for pictures
and therefore for painters. He painted a little himself, and as
he watched Utrillo at work he came to the conclusion that it
was not as difficult as one might think. "I learnt while I watched
him," Gay said modestly. "But I didn't want people to say that
I copied him so I added snow to my paintings."

He was a jovial man. When a client arrived in the bistro
Gay poured out his favourite drink before he had time to order
it. He bought and sold cheap paintings like so many others in
the district. He also sold hams and sausages, and in his window

one often saw hams, paintings and sausages hanging side by side. Utrillo's room overlooked the steps of the rue Mont-Cenis. He led a peaceful, industrious existence at the Casse-Croûte when he was not drinking heavily. Gay had promised Valadon to keep an eye on him, so he did his best to keep him away from the wine. It was said that now and then he locked Utrillo up. Gay denied it. His supervision was not completely successful.

Utrillo found every possible excuse to drink. One night he stamped on the floor until he woke Gay, who came rushing up. Utrillo explained that the smell of zinc white had given him an awful thirst. Would Gay bring up several litres of wine and so save himself the trouble of making several journeys? Gay refused, and returned to the bar where his wife was helping him. Left alone upstairs Utrillo explored the empty flat, even looking into the Gays' bedroom.

"I just can't understand it," Mme. Gay said next morning. "There is not a drop left in the bottle of eau de Cologne."

Utrillo was fond of the ex-policeman, but when the urge to drink became too strong there was no holding him. He would suddenly appear in the bar like one demented, and he was out of the house before Gay could stop him. On such occasions he would stay away for a week or more. He returned looking humble and penitent. "Will you take me back?" he pleaded, and Gay would take him up to his room. On other occasions Gay succeeded in catching him before he could slink away, and had practically to carry him upstairs. The neighbours said he beat Utrillo. Gay denied that too.

Utrillo had generally enough money to pay for wine, for in those days wine cost next to nothing. The rag-and-bone merchants were ready to pay a franc or two for a landscape, and the tavern keepers exchanged wine for paintings, though not every landlord was willing to bargain with him. It is recorded that one turned him down thus:

"Your daubs? What do you want me to do with them? Hang them up? They'd give my wife nightmares."

He was an exception.

Few people retain their sense of humour when in their cups, but Utrillo, who showed very little when sober, could do quite amusing things when tipsy. The trouble was that they were amusing only in his own eyes. Others did not appreciate them.

One night Utrillo vanished. Valadon and Utter were alerted by Gay, and all three searched for him in vain. They never discovered to which bogus dealer or rag-and-bone merchant he had sold the paintings he had taken with him. He was drinking in Low Montmartre, a neighbourhood too extensive for a systematic search. Eventually he bought a case of fireworks, took a room in a hotel and although it was daylight already, proceeded to let off the fireworks in the bedroom. The fire brigade was called and Utrillo escaped with a good thrashing.

His relationship with the police had improved. There was no more *passer à tabac* at the police station: he had to paint pictures for them. If he painted one for a constable, he had to paint two for the sergeant. "The wife," said one policeman to him, "is very fond of views, so make me one." The story has it that to egg him on the sergeant opened bottle after bottle, while Utrillo worked in his temporary studio, the police station.

In 1912, he was making a name for himself in spite of his debauches. Or was it because of them? The late Alfred Bar, who had been professor of art in Paris and who kept aloof from the rowdiness of the Butte, remembered Utrillo during his period with Gay.

"He was a nice person," Bar said, "with enmity toward none. He was, of course, impossible. One couldn't take him out. When I was alone with him he was docile. He was an inexplicable phenomenon. I tried to make him speak of painting. He had little to say about it. He shunned museums and art galleries. If I spoke to him of the great painters of the past, I don't think he even listened. Painting with him was completely instinctive. That doesn't mean that he didn't know his trade. He knew it thoroughly, but there were no aesthetic theories, no dogmas. His drinking didn't interfere with his art. I wonder how he would have painted if a complete cure could have been found for his alcoholism. If he was really raging drunk he would pass me in the street without recognizing me. He had a timid smile when he wasn't too drunk, which I found enchanting."

Bar recollected meeting Utrillo after he had escaped from the Casse-Croûte. He was creeping along by the wall in the rue Mont-Cenis, pretending not to see Bar, who could not resist following him. Utrillo entered the first bistro, looking anxious and worried; when he reached the counter his face lit up and rubbing his hands, he ordered red wine.

Bar was not the only person to like him. In spite of his behaviour, Utrillo managed to keep a few friends, Quizet first among them. Quizet did not live on the Butte and he was seldom present when Utrillo was on the rampage. None the less Quizet knew all about his antics for the Butte was a gossipy village, where your neighbour knew your thoughts before you put them into words. "One couldn't help liking him," Quizet said, "and to watch him painting was a revelation."

Quizet had put it in a nutshell. Utrillo the drunkard was but an irritating, pathetic figure, whereas Utrillo the painter revealed talent amounting to genius. The boozer's escapades distorted the painter's reputation: it was not the drunkard who painted, but the gifted artist. Yet, it *was* the drunkard who created the legend, or inspired others to create it, and ironically it was the legend that brought attention to his painting. None the less, the legend would not be known if Utrillo had not been the outstanding painter he was.

Another friend was Jules Depaquit, who was fourteen years older than Utrillo. Depaquit had tried his hand at watchmaking, house painting and working in an architect's office (his father had been an architect), before running away from his native Sedan. On his arrival in Paris he immediately found his way to the Chat Noir. He drew and wrote poetry, his excellent drawings being much better than his poems. Long before he became well know he illustrated Émile Zola's *Le Rêve*.

He did not take his work too seriously, for all his life he had but one ambition, to have a good time. He loved practical jokes. In the days of the anarchist outrages he denounced himself for having blown up the Restaurant Very in the Boulevard Magenta. He was duly arrested and detained for three days, not because the authorities believed that he had thrown the bomb but because they suspected his sanity. His mother came rushing from Sedan to save him.

He roamed the Butte in slippers, a quaint fellow with an enormous nose and premature grey hair. He was in and out of bistros and always in debt. When he had no money and the desire for drink overtook him he went the round of the bistros carrying a suitcase and announcing that he was returning to Sedan for good. He was entertained everywhere to a farewell drink. When he was carried dead drunk to his room in the Hôtel Bouscarat on the Place du Tertre he was still clinging to his suitcase.

He drew for *Le Journal*, where he was much appreciated.

He was to become the first mayor of the Commune Libre de Montmartre, a self-appointed institution which still flourishes, upheld purely by the importance the Montmartrois attach to themselves. It is typical of the mentality of the Butte that if a true Montmartrois were asked who was the mayor of Montmartre—that is, of the 18th *arrondissement* in 1870—he probably would be quite unaware that it was Georges Clemenceau, but if asked who was the mayor of the Commune Libre in, say, 1921 he would promptly reply: "Why, Jules Depaquit, of course."

Utrillo's friendship with Depaquit began in La Belle Gabrielle, which was the new name of the second tavern that had been called À Ma Campagne. La Belle Gabrielle caused Gay several headaches. It belonged to him, but he had leased it to Marie

Vizier and therefore had no control over it. As La Belle Gabrielle stood at the corner of the rues Mont-Cenis and Saint-Vincent, facing Berlioz's house, it was within easy reach of Utrillo: and Utrillo availed himself of every opportunity that came his way to escape to it. It suited him down to the ground, for the rooms were dark and he could sit unnoticed in a corner, drinking himself silly. If he felt like painting he had the back room at his disposal.

At La Belle Gabrielle Utrillo made friends with another heavy drinker, Georges Tiret-Bognet, who was twenty-eight years his senior. Tiret-Bognet looked like a sergeant major. He had been attached for many years to *L'Illustration* as a sketcher, before photography came in, and he had acquired such ability that with a few strokes he could reproduce any scene his editor wanted. He was a painter too. He scaled no heights and he is now almost forgotten, yet Utrillo considered him a great and important artist.

"Tiret-Bognet? Now that is a great artist," he frequently said, and even in his last years, when most of the art critics were singing Utrillo's praises, he proudly boasted that Tiret-Bognet had said at La Belle Gabrielle: "Your work is out of the ordinary. Work, Maurice, and you'll become first rate."

Utrillo drank in La Belle Gabrielle with the two much older men whenever he succeeded in giving Gay the slip. They had their special table, and later, when Modigliani joined them there, they reminded one of *Los Borrachos* of Velásquez.

If Utrillo became rowdy, Marie Vizier threw him out. He would come back when he escaped again from Gay and ask humbly for forgiveness. Generally, she was more lenient than Frédé. In her tavern he found temporary peace from his enemies and often from himself. He made a painting of La Belle Gabrielle and inscribed it: "Here I spent the happiest days of my life."

Now and then he became jealous of Depaquit because Marie Vizier preferred Depaquit's humourous drawings to Utrillo's oils and water colours. Depaquit made her laugh: Utrillo did not. "He is well known; she sees his drawings in the newspapers," Utrillo muttered. "That is why she prefers him."

"Get out of here," Marie shouted, if the trio became too drunk. Then they went to the Lapin, ordered rum, broke glasses or quarrelled, and were evicted.

Depaquit returned penitent to La Belle Gabrielle. Frequently, homing pigeon that he was, Utrillo staggered back to his mother in the Impasse Guelma, and it took Valadon a couple of days to calm him. On other occasions he went to Tiret-Bognet or Richmond Chaudois, the inventor, who was another friend, in the rue Cortot.

Even in the haven of La Belle Gabrielle, his enemies played a mean trick on him. Marie, who by then had an arrangement with Gay, locked him in the back room with easel, paints and a bottle of wine. Some urchins, always ready to make a fool of Utrillo, passed bottles of wine to him through the window. The usual violent scene followed. He nearly broke down the door and Marie threw him out. A M. Hermann, who had bought a few pictures from him, happened to be in the inn at the time and was witness to the noisy, unedifying scene. When he sobered up Utrillo wanted to find out what M. Hermann's impression of the fracas had been, for he himself could remember little of it. "I believe," he wrote to M. Hermann, "that you were not involved; nevertheless it is absolutely necessary for my fragile moral equilibrium to have your reassurance. Whatever my weaknesses I don't deserve to be despised. What ails me is that they treat me contemptuously at Marie Vizier's." He finished the letter with: "Always good for the grind." It is a pity that M. Hermann's reply, if he did reply, has not been preserved.

Marie Vizier had a new lavatory installed at La Belle Gabrielle, and one morning while she was out Utrillo decided to paint its walls with views of Montmartre. He wanted to give her a pleasant surprise. He worked steadily and the murals were drying by the time she came home. Marie was furious. She was a good-looking though formidable woman and when she shouted one could hear her next door. "You disgusting fellow," she screamed. "You've dirtied my wall."

She found a tin of paraffin and ordered Utrillo to wash it all off. Depaquit and Tiret-Bognet watched him as he cleaned the wall.

"Poor Marie Vizier," wrote Dorgelès. "If only she had kept those pictures and had the walls of her privy framed, her old age would have been secure."

It was said that Utrillo had been in love with Marie Vizier. That does not seem probable considering the attitude he adopted toward women at that time. In his early youth he had run from them: now it was they who ran from him. He insulted women, using the foulest language. He trembled with rage, foamed at the mouth and made threatening gestures if he found himself alone with a woman in the street. The woman would run away and he would run after her with clenched fists.

He shunned all women other than his mother and grandmother. Even as a small boy, he did not take to the servant girls Valadon employed, and was rude to them when they tried to be nice to him. He did not discard his disdain when growing older, for within him he remained a small boy. Those who knew him well at the beginning of the century felt that Utrillo worshiped his mother with such force and respect that he considered all other women unworthy.

"One didn't have to provoke him," said one of the women whom Utrillo had chased. "He provoked himself by working himself into an awful rage. One day we were both on a narrow pavement, he coming toward me. I knew Litrillo's reputation. He stopped and started rolling his eyes, then he made an obscene gesture, so I took to my heels, and he chased me, shouting insults at the top of his voice. I was too nimble for him."

He never ran fast enough to catch any of the women he chased, and it is hard to imagine what would have happened if he had succeeded in doing so. He hated women too much to want any form of physical contact with them—the pursuit was purely symbolic.

The women he chased were always working-class women. No middle-class woman of that time could boast, or complain, that Utrillo had molested her. The only exceptions perhaps were pregnant women. He felt a deep antagonism toward them and wanted to kick them in the belly. He really meant to do so, yet, however heavily pregnant the women were, they all appear to have run faster than Utrillo. There is no record of any having come to harm.

A concierge in the rue Lepic once fired a pistol at Utrillo. She missed. She was arrested and taken to the police station, where she admitted that he had not harmed her but that she had listened to his "perfidious suggestions" and had shot at him "to make the people of the Butte believe that he was dangerously mad." She was released.

Valadon believed that her son was impotent. In those days that was as final as being castrated. An impotent person had, as it were, no more right of appeal than a eunuch. True, she cherished hopes that if the right girl were found he would shake off his impotence like influenza. She employed a model called Gaby and thought her a very nice girl; so she decided that Gaby was the right girl for Utrillo. She brought them together. The idyll, if it was an idyll, lasted for two days, then Gaby fled. Even Valadon did not see her again. There was no more talk of finding a wife for Maurice. Valadon was reticent about the reasons that caused Gaby's abrupt departure.

"He isn't made for marriage," was her comment.

According to some chroniclers, Utrillo did have a few adventures with low prostitutes of Montmartre, which ended each time in a noisy scene with the ponce coming to the damsel's rescue and beating Utrillo up. He had, he told Carco, once gone to live with a working-class woman, but that lasted only a few days. "It could have worked," Utrillo said, "if she hadn't drunk, the bitch." Carco could hardly believe his ears.

Utrillo lived in a world where women were always available. The Butte abounded in them; his friends and acquaintances all had their mistresses and changed them when the fancy took them, for it was easy to pick and choose. When he went drinking farther afield—that is, to Low Montmartre—he was surrounded in the streets and cafés by prostitutes and the like. Wherever he looked he saw women who were neither housewives nor upholders of virtue. In the Place Clichy, which he frequented, there was a *brasserie* almost reserved, so to speak, for female absinthe drinkers. In winter they grouped themselves round the brazier on the terrace, in poses much liked by Degas, dressed as in the prints of Toulouse-Lautrec or the water colours of Bottini. They wore English coats with large checks, hats with plumes or flowers of a past fashion. Their make-up was black and red, and some of them still spoke of the late "Monsieur Toulouse."

Utrillo liked watching them. Years later he would bring them up in conversation. Standing in the snow and observing them huddled round the brazier, he must have felt some kinship with them. Yet he never spoke to any of them.

2

Utrillo's impressionist period lasted for two years, 1905 and 1906; the white period from 1907 to 1908. After 1908, as Tabarant put it, came the apogee. Up to 1908 he painted between six and seven hundred paintings without figures, most of them on cardboard of various thicknesses. In 1905, when he was twenty-two, he had begun to sign his pictures "Maurice, Utrillo, V." Before that he had started with "Maurice Valadon," and then "M. U. Valadon." It was during his first two phases that his art found its personality. He discovered what landscape painters had not suspected before, namely the life of houses.

Houses meant the same to him as nudes meant to Rubens, Fragonard and Renoir. His houses were as naked as their nudes. He isolated them or let them group themselves along a street. His windows had secretive eyes.

The object of his painting was the houses. The streets were subservient to them, and since most of the houses he painted were Montmartre houses, and the streets they dominated were the winding streets of the Butte, it was not difficult to find buyers for them. Montmartre is and was a symbol for the many, the symbol of something like nostalgia, a lump in the throat, intangible yet positively present. Today on the Place du Tertre the outdoor painters, whose easels stand side by side in rows and who work like a factory team, all manage to find buyers for their Montmartre landscapes. Some sell over seven hundred landscapes a year.

The first art dealer to buy Utrillo's work was Anzoli. Anzoli had been frame maker to Degas, Lautrec, Paul Signac and Mary Cassatt. Valadon used to sell him drawings, and, since he was a mean man and she lacked commercial sense, Anzoli was pleased with her. She showed him some of her son's paintings and Anzoli took a few, exchanging them for frames. Frames were not what Utrillo needed: he could not barter frames for drink. He preferred to sell his paintings for a few francs to the second-hand dealers who bought pictures as a sideline. They conducted their business leaning against the wall of L'Abbaye de Thélème in the Place Pigalle, their goods displayed in open sheds. Serat, a rag-and-bone man, and Jacobi, an ex-butcher, were among the first to buy Utrillos. Tabarant, who was to do so much to help Utrillo achieve fame, bought his first Utrillo from Jacobi. It was a painting of the Eiffel Tower. However, the first serious dealer in Utrillos was Soulier.

Soulier lived in the rue des Martyrs, facing Medrano's circus. He had a powerful frame, black curly hair, and rosy cheeks which came not from the fresh air but the fifty or so drinks he took daily. He paid his bill twice a day, remembering how many drinks he had had. He spoke calmly, giving the impression of a deep thinker, and had a slow, ponderous gait. If he was not in his shop he could be found in the nearby bistro of *Père* Pabot: and it was advisable to take him to the bistro before talking business. He had started life as a prizefighter. When he retired from the ring he sold mattresses and bedsteads, but one day he exchanged a mattress for a painting and the passion for dealing in pictures seized him. Soon his shop was crowded with canvases brought to him by the *rapins* of the Butte. He never refused an oil painting or a water colour. He paid between twenty-five centimes and a few francs for them, and when the deal was clinched he treated the seller to a drink in the bistro.

He lived above his shop. As his passion grew, the space in his bedroom shrank. Eventually he could not get to his bed because of the canvases that blocked the way, so he had to sleep in a hotel. Drinking one night in the bistro, he forgot to go back and lock his door, leaving this thousand or so pictures at the mercy of an intruder. Not one picture was stolen, but the dogs of the neighbourhood went upstairs to lift their legs against the canvases.

Soulier thought that every picture he bought was a Manet. Manet for him was the greatest of all painters. Whenever he bought a painting he said: "This time I am sure it is a Manet." He never found a Manet though once he did buy a Renoir for forty francs. He talked big; he had bought and sold the works of all the great masters. He dropped names like Goya, Murillo and Rubens and claimed that Picasso, Van Dongen and Douanier Rousseau were among his customers. Utrillo liked dealing with Soulier because of the drink he gave him whenever he bought a picture. The price for the picture was two francs. For the princely sum of two francs, Coquiot observed, Utrillo would have painted all the streets of Paris and Montmagny.

Valadon and doctors had thought that painting would keep

Utrillo's mind off the bottle: but it was painting that provided him with the bottles his insatiable thirst required.

Clovis Sagot, who was known as Clovis the madman, was Utrillo's next buyer after Soulier. He had begun his working life as a journeyman baker. He was a man who followed his impulses and predilections, and when he had graduated into art dealing he concentrated on buying and selling paintings by the Fauves—Matisse, Derain, Vlaminck and Othon Friesz among them. They were called Fauves because they had had their first exhibition at the Cage des Fauves in 1909. Soulier favoured the Fauves to annoy his brother Edmond, a print merchant, who was not an admirer of the movement.

Sagot had an eye for paintings, which was more than one could say of Soulier, though he had little business sense. When Utrillo came to see him for the first time he was well received. Sagot addressed him as *toi* right away and said: "You certainly have something in your belly, but you are too much influenced by Sisley and Pissarro. Get rid of their influence. Drink less and work more."

Utrillo saw no reason why he should drink less since no painter could be more prolific than he. Sagot upbraided him for not using enough colours. "Bolt down the colours," he said. He was convinced that the strange young man would go a long way. "One day you will be the richest of us all," he prophesied.

Sagot sold Utrillos at five to ten francs apiece between 1909 and 1912. He sent some to Switzerland, where a few were sold at around fifteen to twenty francs. The first foreign exhibition in which Utrillo appeared was in 1912 in Munich (Die Neue Kunst, Hans Goltz, Odeonplatz), where paintings were also exhibited by Cézanne, Van Gogh, Gauguin, Braque, Picasso, Derain, Van Dongen, Delaunay, Le Fauconnier, Roussel, Vlaminck, Matisse, Valadon, Herbin and Marchand. Utrillo was represented by a *Rue du Chevalier de la Barre* and a *Steps of the Sacré-Coeur*. Sagot asked a hundred francs each; he had paid

Utrillo thirty francs for the two. Neither of them was sold. His dealings with Soulier and Sagot did not stop Utrillo from continuing to flog his paintings outside L'Abbaye de Thélème. When in need of money for drink—he had practically no other needs—he sold to anyone at any price. Among his early clients was the actor Dorival, from the Comédie Française, an art collector and one of the first private persons, other than a tavern keeper or secondhand dealer, who sensed the importance of Utrillo's paintings.

They had met in 1909 and for five to ten francs Dorival bought some of the finest white-period pictures, among them a *Moulin de la Galette*, a *Maison de Berlioz* and a *Rue des Abbesses*. Dorival was perhaps the first to acquire Utrillos with figures, mostly anemic little fellows seen from behind. Utrillo regarded his Maecenas in a simple, straightforward fashion: Dorival existed in order to keep him in drink. If he was in need of wine he painted a picture, which he took to Dorival before the paint was dry. Thirst has no timetable, so Utrillo turned up at any hour of the day or night at Dorival's home in the Boulevard de Clichy, bullying or begging if the actor was not in the mood to buy. Utrillo could be very insistent.

Their relationship lasted until 1911, when they fell out. Dorival had tired of being wakened in the middle of the night. He wanted no more Utrillos. Utrillo wrote Dorival a rude letter, accusing him of having used defamatory expressions about his paintings. It is interesting to note that he defended the paintings, though it was the artist whom Dorival objected to. Dorival kept all the paintings, of course, but ignored the painter's letter.

Utrillo again rang Dorival's bell at night. When Dorival refused to open the door Utrillo stormed into the courtyard of the block of flats, shouting: "Here are the scavengers!" or "*Merde pour Dorival!*" One night Utrillo made such a disturbance on the staircase that the concierge came out with a pistol. Some of the tenants joined him. Utrillo continued yelling

for Dorival. He had brought two canvases and he needed money.
The concierge and his companions called to Dorival to come
down. Utrillo went on shouting. They started up the stairs,
but Utrillo was nimbler. He reached the sixth floor when they
were still at the third and made water on them from the landing.

After this incident Utrillo decided that it was preferable to
work with dealers. Libaude succeeded Soulier as his dealer. After
the butcher, the journeyman baker and the mattress maker came
the auctioneer, who specialized in the sale of horses. Libaude
had managed *Art Littéraire* for a while. The names of Fargue
and Jarry were mentioned in print in *Art Littéraire* for the
first time. With Émile Bernard, who lived at 12 rue Cortot,
Libaude started *La Rénovation Esthétique* and still found time
for horses and paintings. He was a man of parts.

He looked like an undertaker. He was rapacious and something of a bully, yet, said Francis Jourdain, the distinguished
painter, illustrator and decorator, he would not have harmed a
flea. His skin was a sickly green. He had a flat in the rue Baudin
which he turned into an office and gallery. Every afternoon
he slunk into the Hôtel de Ventes in the rue Drouot, now the
Hôtel de Drouot and the most important auction room in Paris,
gave a quick, furtive glance at the paintings to be auctioned,
then vanished like a shadow. "I should like to have a chat with
you," he said one day to Tabarant. "Where could I see you? I
would invite you to luncheon if I hadn't kidney trouble. My
stomach is in a bad state and my liver in a real mess."

Libaude took exception to the way in which Utrillo signed
his paintings. He scrawled his name in too large letters and, in
spite of Libaude's remonstrations, continued to do so. Libaude
appealled to Valadon, who solved the problem in a simple
manner: she signed "Maurice, Utrillo, V," in neat, small letters
in the right-hand bottom corner of the canvases.

Libaude had already been in touch with Valadon in July
1909. He had written to her about one of Utrillo's canvases.
"As I have had no news from my friend Émile Bernard,"

wrote Libaude, "I do not know whether he gave you my message.

"I asked him to tell you that I am willing to buy a painting by your son, *Cathédrale de Paris*, which I saw at Sagot's for the price of fifty francs.

"This might seem moderate to you but his paintings have already been offered to me by another dealer.

"It will, of course, be necessary to see the painting again and see that it is the same one so as to avoid confusion.

"The price I offer is *strictly between us*. I hardly buy the works of the *young* any more, though I am willing to make an exception with your son as I am specially interested in his talent."

Libaude pushed Utrillo's work seriously and forcefully. He paid him twenty francs a painting and then tried to sell it for fifty. It was not easy to work with Utrillo. Firstly, Utrillo was always willing to sell to anybody even when he was under contract; secondly, he painted more than Libaude needed; and thirdly, Libaude, the horse dealer, was not always satisfied with his work.

"Utrillo's dry style grieves me," he wrote to Utter, who was generally present when Utrillos were sold. "One should persuade him to rely less on the ruler when he draws. Everybody reproaches him with his dryness of style."

"Since the first days of April," Libaude wrote to Utrillo on April 18, 1912, "you have brought me a painting every two days. That is far too much and I fear that your hasty work can only harm you. I don't think one can acquire a serious reputation without working strenuously."

Still, Libaude could not complain: nobody knew better than he that he was underpaying Utrillo, as the following example shows.

Manzana Pissarro had left his house in the rue Choron on an April day, when a sudden cloudburst sent him to seek shelter in a doorway. The sons of Camille Pissarro were well-dressed, distinguished-looking men, not given to hobnobbing with the dissolute, yet a tall young man, none too clean or tidy looking,

came and sheltered beside Manzana. The young man carried several paintings which he put against the wall. Manzana, the
painter, could not resist glancing in their direction.

"Very good paintings," he exclaimed. "Who painted them?"

"I did."

"You?" asked Manzana incredulously.

"Yes, and they're for sale. Dirt cheap."

Manzana looked at them again, then asked if he had heard of
Camille Pissarro.

"Pissarro," cried Utrillo. "What a great painter! Why do you
ask me?"

Manzana explained that he was his son. Utrillo told him of
that swine of a Sagot who usually paid five francs and now
wanted no more paintings from him, and of another swine,
named Libaude, who did not pay much either.

"Bring these pictures to me," Manzana said. "Here's my address. I'll sell them for you at a much better price."

At five the next morning Manzana was wakened by loud banging on his door, alerting the whole household. Utrillo burst in
completely drunk. He had brought ten paintings with him. He
fell against a chest of drawers and collapsed. Manzana and his
wife got him on his feet again. It was not easy. "Ask ten francs
for each of them," Utrillo mumbled, "and we'll go half and
half."

Manzana assured him that he wanted nothing for himself.
Utrillo staggered off and Manzana sent for Libaude, who came
humbly to the great Camille's son, a good painter in his own
right, and bought the lot at fifty francs each. He would have
paid only twenty francs to Utrillo. On the following day Manzana handed over five hundred francs and Utrillo could not believe his eyes. It was the biggest sum he had ever seen. Manzana
could not believe that the unkempt, hirsute young man had
really painted those excellent pictures. He asked Utrillo to bring
his brushes and palette and paint something in his presence.

A pickled herring was sticking out of Utrillo's pocket. "A

pickled herring," Utrillo explained, "makes you even thirstier."
Manzana stood beside him while he mixed his colours with the
bravura of a true artist. Now Manzana believed that Utrillo
himself had painted those landscapes.

A few days later Valadon called on Manzana, who had never
met her, though her reputation had reached him. She went
straight to the point and begged Manzana not to give Utrillo
any more money, for he was still riotously drunk on the five
hundred francs.

Manzana promised. He had no occasion to keep his word as
Utrillo never came back.

Utrillo had been painting churches and cathedrals since 1909.
It would be moving to be able to say that the painter found his
faith in God while he painted churches, that his brush lifted
him, as it were, to God. But Utrillo had found his own form of
religion well before he took to painting cathedrals and churches.
He painted them because he believed in God. In his case the
beauty of his cathedrals and churches was in the eye of the believer. After all, one is not inspired by one's work: it is the other
way about.

While Utrillo was still in Montmagny his grandmother gave
him a catechism to read. She hoped it would keep him quiet for
half an hour or so. He read it first like any reading matter without knowing what it meant. In some inscrutably dark corner of
his mind a light must have been lit, for he read it again and
again as a child reads a fairy tale. Eventually the pages became
so torn and dirty that Madeleine had to replace it with a new
one. He made little sense of the Ten Commandments; mortal sin
did not worry him. All he retained, and he retained that for life,
was his veneration for the Blessed Virgin. Joan of Arc, whom he
had first met in the church of Notre-Dame-de-Clignancourt,
came next in his heart.

Valadon, the fervent anticlerical, welcomed his progress toward God. She had not given up hope that some influence

stronger than drink would one day possess her son. She consulted a doctor, who said: "Very good idea, make him religious."

In Montmagny she did not dare to send him to church because the congregation was aware of his scandalous reputation. It never occurred to anyone to have him baptized. And Utrillo did not wish it either, firstly because he had not taken in the meaning of baptism, and secondly because he felt that praying and painting churches would satisfy the Holy Trinity.

In Montmartre he was allowed to go to mass. That was before he left the rue Cortot for the first time. He went to the red brick church of St. John the Baptist in the rue des Abbesses, the ugliest church in Paris, known locally as St. John of the Bricks. Valadon gave him three sous, one for the chair, one for the collection, and one for himself. One Sunday she forgot to give him the three sous, and he did not think of them until time came for the collection. He searched his pockets in vain. Shaking with rage, he shouted and gesticulated. Mass was interrupted while he was led out.

Valadon had often to buy him new missals, for in his zeal he tore out pages as he tried to follow the mass. His missals were those published for children. In the draughty church of St. John the Baptist a leaf of his torn missal was blown away during a sung mass when the church was full. The leaf came to rest in front of the chair of a fat old woman. There was a crowd of fat old women in the church. Utrillo saw the leaf drop and he wanted it back: it was his property. He went down on all fours in order not to interrupt the mass or make himself conspicuous, and crawled under the chairs in an attempt to retrieve it. The result was that he tipped several fat old women off their seats and created uproar and scandal.

After that incident he went only to early mass in some small out-of-the-way church, though even there he became fidgety and nervous if anyone were present except the priest and server.

Utter said he oscillated between revering a mystic St. Joan of Arc and a romantic d'Artagnan. He thought in emotions, not in concepts. If Utter felt like annoying him he said that Joan of Arc was a peasant girl surrounded by coarse soldiers and that she used their language.

"Utrillo would prefer to paint huge Joans of Arc instead of landscapes," Utter observed. "Luckily the painter in him stops him from that."

Utrillo was eventually baptized in 1935 when he was fifty-two. Yet faith had as little effect on his drinking habits as painting.

Valadon and Utter had returned to 12 rue Cortot in 1910. They took the studio on the second floor, but with Mousis no longer there to foot the bills they led a hand-to-mouth existence. Utrillo commuted, so to speak, between the rue Cortot and Gay's establishment. From time to time he stayed with Marie Vizier at La Belle Gabrielle. He was becoming worse. One drunken bout followed another; he kept the Montmartre police pretty busy. When his mother went one morning to bail him out the commissioner of police told her bluntly that if he had more trouble with her son he would send him to prison. Utrillo had become so aggressive when drunk that he would tiptoe into a café, stealthily approach the peaceful *belote* players, fling their cards in the air, and with a loud shout, sweep the glasses off the counter. There was, Valadon realized, only one way out, namely to put him into a nursing home and make him undergo another cure. Both she and Utrillo were beginning to take nursing homes as part and parcel of Utrillo's life: she still believing in a complete cure, he taking them, so to speak, in his stride. But the trouble was that neither she nor Utter had the money to pay for it. Libaude appeared to be their only answer, but his reputation for meanness had reached them also.

They went to see him. Fear or timidity had never handicapped Valadon or Utter. They took Utrillo along. Utrillo was always willing to co-operate when in a chastised, docile mood, and then he was the first to long to be cured. Libaude received them coldly, bade them sit down at a table in the middle of the room and then seated himself at the head of it.

"*La séance est ouverte*," said Chairman Libaude in a loud voice to show them that he had the situation firmly in hand. Valadon wanted to speak. "It is for your son to speak," said Libaude haughtily. It was Utter who spoke first.

"Libaude was a nasty little man," Utter said years later. Whenever his name cropped up in the bistros of the Place du Tertre, Utter would glare and frown as if Libaude were taking a drink at the other end of the bar. "One had to hit him hard below the belt. I mastered him because I knew how to shout him down."

When Utter had spoken, Libaude agreed to pay for the cure. Though Utter was convinced that he had browbeaten him, Libaude had enough business acumen to appreciate that the required medical attention was actually a first-class business proposition. Without it, Utrillo might cease to be such a source of profit. Utter and Valadon asked for three hundred francs a month.

"Three hundred francs a month?" screamed Libaude. "I would be taken for a lunatic if I paid that sum."

Utter threatened to get the money from another dealer. Libaude was too avaricious to risk even such a slight possibility. He agreed to pay the amount, if Utrillo undertook to paint a number of pictures each week while the cure lasted. Libaude provided the measurements and subjects. Utrillo went to Dr. Revertégat's nursing home in the Avenue Rozée in Sannois, where Libaude visited him once a week to collect the paintings.

Before the 1914–18 war, and for some time after, the cure for alcoholics still was a very unscientific affair. The patients were merely kept away from drink and segregated from the drinking population. The doctors had a simple approach to the problem: if the alcoholic were forced to accustom himself to a drinkless existence he would lose the need for it. They overlooked the psychological factors; in fact, it was not yet fashionable to consider them. If a patient became demented by lack of alcohol then small doses of it were squirted into his veins, though only rarely. When the doctors found that the patient had accustomed himself to going without alcohol he was allowed to go.

Utrillo's behaviour was exemplary in the nursing home. He went out of his way to prove to doctors and nurses that drink was his sole trouble, because, as he said afterward, you never knew in such establishments. He was not mad, he told all, only an alcoholic. He wanted to get out as soon as possible and so he took care to do nothing that might give the impression that he was abnormal. He tried to persuade the male nurse who looked after him to take him near the inn where he could paint in the shade. The nurse would not play. While in Sannois, Utrillo painted some exceptionally fine landscapes. It was a warm spring and Utrillo knew how to put tender foliage on canvas.

Utrillo left Sannois completely cured again. He was twenty-seven years old. Doctor and nurses were pleased with him; he was pleased with himself. Valadon, Utter and Gay awaited him with open arms, yet he was to go back into Sannois only eight months later.

Figures were appearing in almost all his paintings. Utrillo was a landscape painter, pure but not simple. He rarely painted still lifes. Around 1912 he tried his hand at cactuses, and later at flowers—neither added to his glory, both lacked his personality. They had no distinction. One cannot but wonder why figures became important for him.

The figures that people his canvases from 1910 onward are lifeless patches of colour, and the dimensions are usually all wrong in relation to the buildings. The figures are unwanted, unnecessary, gauche creatures who have nothing to say for themselves, and they appear to have nowhere to go. It has been said by Tabarant and other art critics that those figures have a profound psychological meaning. They were, they thought, his revenge on society because he could not accept its standards.

He did a painting of his arrest outside La Belle Gabrielle. There the figures should have mattered. In that picture he could have revenged himself on the police by making them look ridiculous. They look like marionettes.

After he had left Sannois he painted the barracks at Compiègne. The gate is closed, a sentry in red trousers stands in the sentry box, the tricolour flutters over the locked gate, trees are visible on the other side of the wall, and there is a red restaurant to the left. Three lifeless couples stand near the restaurant and one wonders what brought them there. A woman with huge buttocks, a forerunner of all his women, faces the sentry. If one wants to read meaning into that picture one finds it in the closed gate and the walled-in trees rather than in the figures.

He painted the rue de la Jonquière, a mournful street of the poor, with soulless houses. In the middle of the street a horse is drawing a solitary cab; only the back of the cab and the horse's hooves are visible yet one feels that the poor animal is undernourished. The houses threaten to close in on horse and cab.

Utrillo had begun to paint from postcards. There has been a good deal written about this. Some critics have accused him of being an "anti-painter" since no conscientious artist, they maintain, would paint in this manner. Others claim that painting from postcards is preferable to using a hurried sketch.

But the technique was purely for functional reasons. When he painted out of doors on the Butte he usually came to grief. He would leave his easel in search of drink, or, if he was broke, in search of someone to buy him a drink. At times, once he had started to drink he forgot canvas and easel. When he staggered out of the bistro he could not find his easel again. It had vanished. Next morning his mother would look for him at the police station.

When this became an almost daily habit Valadon had an inspiration. "Paint from postcards," she said, "that will be less trouble." So he took to painting from postcards because it was less dangerous than painting out of doors on the Butte.

The postcards were ordinary black and white photographic reproductions. They jogged his memory and that was all. If he wanted to paint a certain street or square he painted it really from memory, the postcards reminding him of details he might momentarily have forgotten. Thus he would paint a street with the buildings of yesterday. He would paint, say, the rue Mont-Cenis with houses that had been pulled down several years before, and without the new ones that had since been built. In 1947 he was to paint the rue Norvins as it had looked in 1915. The postcard he used to refresh his memory was pinned to the wall as he worked. Some of the postcards were perforated by dozens of small holes made with drawing pins.

Delacroix, Cézanne and Derain among many others painted now and then from engravings. The postcards, admittedly inferior to engravings, served the same purpose for Utrillo. He used a compass, ruler, square and T square when working. He started off by measuring distances like an architect, then came the drawing, and then he painted as though the postcard were the forbidden street itself.

Utrillo made M. Gilbert Gruet of the Bernheim-Jeune Gallery of Paris a present of a postcard which represented the Impasse Traînée. The holes showed that he had often made use of it. The word *Neige* was written on it. He had written the word on the post card to remind himself that the Impasse Traînée should always be painted in the snow.

Utrillo achieved such facility using postcards as models that he could paint a landscape after a postcard of any street in any town. Émile Bernard gave him one with a view of Toulouse and asked him to make a painting from it. Utrillo obliged. The painting went into the Henri Lapauze collection.

"With those things," Utrillo said of postcards, "one cannot go wrong." And when someone laughed at him because he painted in this way, "Try it and you'll find out for yourself," he replied.

3

"Paulo, Frédé's second son, wanted to murder me," Utrillo used to declare of Paulo of the Lapin Agile, with the flair for exaggeration and drama inherited from his mother. The truth was that Valadon had begged Paulo not to allow Utrillo into the Lapin when he was drunk but to send him home. So whenever Utrillo entered drunk, Paulo waved his arms and made hissing noises. "As with a chicken," Paulo said.

The writers and painters of the Butte hunted, so to speak, in packs. Utrillo belonged only to Depaquit and Tiret-Bognet's group, whereas Depaquit went out also with Fornerod, Picasso, Girieud, Asselin and Delaw. There was a Spanish group led by Manolo Huguet, the sculptor. The members were Durrio, Canals, Sunyer, Etchevarria, Zuloaga and Picasso. Georges Delaw had a second gang consisting of Charles Laborde, Asselin, Jacques Vaillant and Capy. Pierre Mac Orlan, Daragnès, Heuzé, Warnod, Caillé, Girieud, Max Jacob and Apollinaire formed another coterie. Derain, Vlaminck and Salmon belonged to Max Jacob's second pack. The lists show poignantly Utrillo's isolation in a world bursting with talent and gaiety.

One night Max Jacob found a shape covered with snow in the rue des Saules. It had evidently come from the Lapin and it could only be Utrillo. Max Jacob dug him out and offered to escort him home, but Utrillo was afraid to go home, fearing that Utter would give him a beating. Utter beat Utrillo when he was violently drunk. "For his own good," said Utter. Max Jacob took him to his own room where there was only one bed. With exquisite politeness the host inquired which side of the bed his guest preferred. Utrillo chose the side nearer the wall. Utrillo showed his gratitude by telling anyone who was willing to listen that he had chosen the wall because he was afraid Jacob would make amorous advances to him.

Most of the painters and writers of the Lapin Agile had their studios in the Bateau-Lavoir, the Washing Barge. The name had been invented by Max Jacob because the house reminded him of the creaking, old washing barges on the Seine. The building rocked too, Jacob maintained. One of the first inmates was Van Dongen. Picasso came to live there in 1904 in the company of Manolo Huguet and Gonzalès, another Spanish sculptor. On their heels came Louis Markous, known as Marcoussis. Severini and Modigliani shared the same studio and their neighbours at different times were Georges Kars, Derain, Braque, Galanis, Marie Laurencin, Maria Blanchard, Juan Gris, Picabia, Friesz, Raoul Dufy, Alfred Jarry, Pierre Mac Orlan, Gustave Coquiot, Francis Carco, Max Jacob, André Warnod and Apollinaire. Utrillo told Pedro Creixams, the Spanish-Catalan painter, that he had never set foot in the Bateau-Lavoir. However, his mother and stepfather often went there.

The famous banquet for Douanier Rousseau was given in Picasso's studio in 1907. Apollinaire read his homage:

Tu te souviens Rousseau du paysage aztèque . . .

Braque played the accordion. Gertrude Stein, her brother Leo and Alice B. Toklas were among the guests. Jacques Vaillant chewed soap in the hope that when it began to froth the Americans would think that he had delirium tremens which, anyway, would not have been considered exceptional in that company. Shortly before midnight Max Jacob and André Salmon put the tipsy father of the naïfs into a cab. "After that," wrote Mino Frank, "the party became overtly Montmartrois."

The Place Ravignan, the quiet little square with trees in front of the Bateau-Lavoir, was in time renamed Place Émile Goudeau after the founder of the Hydropathes. Bruant and Utrillo have their streets in Montmartre, Valadon and Goudeau their squares, only Rodolphe Salis of the Chat Noir is forgotten, yet he brought the art of wit to the hillock of the martyrs.

During his stay in the Bateau-Lavoir Carco decided to call

on Gay. He had, of course, seen Utrillo in the Lapin but had not spoken with him. Gay took him up to Utrillo's room which was furnished with only a bed, a chair, a looking glass and an easel. A lone, bare electric bulb hung from the ceiling. Utrillo was drawing when Gay led Carco in. Gay introduced Carco ceremoniously; Utrillo did not speak. Utrillo, Gay explained, worked too much. Your throat becomes parched if you work too hard, and the smell of turpentine and zinc white is the real begetter of thirst. Utrillo nodded his approval.

Gay asked Utrillo whether Carco could glance at the canvas. Utrillo looked anxiously at Carco but remained silent. After they had left, Gay spoke of him as Monsieur Maurice. If he used the name Utrillo, Gay whispered, Utrillo would come rushing down. Gay showed Carco his own paintings. On the backs of the canvases Utrillo had written: "Good" or "Passable" or "My compliments to my best pupil."

Gay went on to say that Utrillo always behaved bashfully at a first meeting. Next time Carco should address him as Monsieur Maurice. He became affable if called by his Christian name, for that reminded him of his childhood when life had been much easier for him. If he, Gay, called him Utrillo he became intractable. "You have no idea, but if I called him Utrillo he would start drinking straight away."

Yet Utrillo when sober was not continuously sad and solemn. In the right-hand corner of one of his many paintings of the Moulin de la Galette he wrote: "Factory of Artistic Paintings. Landscapes a Speciality. First-class Colours—Maurice Utrillo, V, 12 rue Cortot, Paris 18e. Beware of Imitations." But that was, one might say, just a joke between Utrillo and Monsieur Maurice.

His dread of people, which lashed him to a fury, did not desert him when he visited art galleries. Francis Jourdain happened to be in the Druet Gallery one morning when Utrillo came in trying to sell a landscape. He was under contract to Libaude, though such trifles did not worry him if he was in need of drink.

He looked dissolute. Druet had long ago lost faith in human wrecks. He hardly glanced at the painting.

"It is quite good," Jourdain interjected.

Druet's accountant, who was present, asked him whether he would really pay fifty francs for the picture. Jourdain persuaded Druet to buy it, and all he received as commission was a furious look from Utrillo. Still, they had met.

The next time Jourdain saw Utrillo's work was at Libaude's. He went there, in 1913, with Elie Faure, and Libaude showed him his collection of Utrillos. He asked two hundred francs for a landscape because, he explained, he seldom found buyers for Utrillo's paintings. Jourdain chose two Montmagny landscapes at the usual price of fifty francs. He showed them to Druet who remained cold. He had the same reaction from Eugène Blot, who was usually enthusiastic about young artists. Undeterred, Jourdain took Paul Gallimard to Libaude, and he bought several paintings. Jourdain persuaded his father and brother-in-law to buy Utrillos. The great day came when he took Octave Mirbeau to Libaude and the great man there met Utrillo in person.

Now Mirbeau was a writer. He had the imagination and fertility of the novelist, and both were fired by the stories about Utrillo. It was too good to be true, therefore the author of L'Abbé Jules, Le journal d'une femme de chambre, Dingo and other works decided to make it even better. He bought Utrillo's La maison rose and hung it up in his drawing room among other fine paintings. Then he gave full rein to his imagination. He showed the painting and subsequent paintings he had bought to his literary friends, exclaiming: "Hurry, buy his work quickly. There won't be many more to come. I had to tear these paintings out of his hands. He wanted to destroy them. The man is completely mad . . . . He hadn't eaten for eight days when I bought that picture." He pointed to La maison rose. "He drinks methylated spirits, but he is a genius." He had found Utrillo, so he explained, in a Montmartre attic, foaming at the mouth, yet painting steadily. He saw him rolling on the floor, wanting to set fire to the attic.

His high praise of the paintings and the stories he invented set the ball rolling and it has not stopped rolling since. His friends went to Libaude to see the paintings of the frothing, methylated spirits-drinking, epileptic madman who had little time left on earth, yet was a genius. Libaude himself came to Mirbeau, offering to buy back *La maison rose*.

"Nothing doing," laughed Mirbeau. "They offer me a fortune for the painting, but I promised Utrillo to give it back to him. Otherwise he will never paint again."

Started by Mirbeau in 1913, Utrillo and the legend were launched together.

Utrillo was the perfect medium for a legend. His alcoholism and buffoon-like behaviour coupled with his extraordinary talent could not but fire the imagination of a writer and man like Mirbeau; and because Utrillo had no sense of shame, no social sensibilities, one could write of him whatever one wanted without fear of libel action. Utrillo's legend was established before he reached the age of thirty. He did remarkably well from it. So did the writers. "If you can't think of a new subject then all you have to do is to write about Utrillo," Carco observed.

There is not one book about Utrillo, not one preface to his paintings, which does not lay excessive stress on his scandalous drinking, rowdiness, desire to kick pregnant women and his sojourns in mental hospitals. Those books and prefaces were all written during Utrillo's lifetime. In 1921, for instance, when Carco wrote a critical essay on Utrillo's paintings in *Le Carnet des Artistes* he considered himself called upon to mention his "somber habit of drinking."

The legend did not ask for accuracy. In one of his books Carco stated that Utrillo was an absinthe drinker.

"WINE! The author is infamous albeit my friend," wrote Utrillo in the margin. The word wine was three times underlined.

That was his only objection. The next time he met Carco he did not even mention the small inaccuracy.

"My son blushes only in anger," Valadon said. Utrillo was sorry if he hurt his mother, yet did not regret his rowdy public behaviour. One cannot put the blame on drink alone. There are plenty of alcoholics who drink to bury their sense of shame and guilt. Utrillo simply lacked such feelings. Therefore, he found nothing extraordinary in the written accounts of his excesses. He drank himself silly on wine but not on absinthe. That was all.

Shortly after Utrillo and the legend had been launched Valadon went to call on Francis Jourdain. With tears in her eyes she thanked him for all he had done for her son. Jourdain did not understand why she was so effusive. It occurred to him only after she had left that the "unfortunate woman," as he put it, imagined that success would be the saving of her terrible son, and money would open the doors of the nursing homes that cured rich alcoholics.

"She was dreaming," Jourdain added.

Holidays, War and Modigliani

1

TIME, the great appeaser, did not improve Utrillo's relations
with Libaude in spite of the frequent payments the art
dealer made to the nursing home whenever Utrillo needed a cure.
Libaude would have preferred to see him locked up for good.
When Utrillo was at large he did not respect their verbal agreement but sold his paintings to all and sundry. In a sense this
was encouraged by Libaude, who made it a principle to refuse
a certain number of his pictures. On one occasion he lost an out-
standingly fine painting of a church of the white period. His
meanness often got the better of his rapacity. Moreover, he refused to enter into a written agreement. Still, he supplied
Utrillo with enough pocket money for drink and paints in the
years leading up to the First World War.

Valadon would not let matters rest either. Though she lacked
commercial sense, she was a great enough artist to appreciate the

value of a work of art, the toil, sweat, struggle and disappoint-
ment that went into the execution of a good painting. She was
not one to beat about the bush: small and slender though she
was, she did not hesitate when she thought herself called upon
to take the bull by the horns. She rushed to the attack, threatening Libaude that she would tell everyone how badly he paid
her son.

"I received a menacing letter from Mme. Valadon," wrote
Libaude to Utrillo on May 14, 1912. "She speaks of divulging
the price I pay you . . . I feel it is my duty to tell you that
if she carries her threat into effect I shall not buy any more paintings from you."

Valadon did not divulge the price he paid for Utrillos, for
suddenly she needed Libaude. Utrillo had taken to stealing his
mother's drawings when he was thirsty and had no work of his
own to sell. He sold them to secondhand dealers, accepting
any small amount for them. Valadon had hidden a number of
his early studies at Montmagny; her intention was to keep them
as mementos of his early paintings. Afraid that he would find
and sell them too, she took all forty of them to Libaude who
bought them for the magnificent sum of a hundred francs, fifty
sous apiece. The money was safer with her, she believed, since
she didn't drink, yet she squandered it. One needed the strength
of a Libaude to stand up to mother and son. He was always
game to take advantage of them however impossibly and in-
consistently they behaved.

Utrillo was in and out of trouble all the time. One day a friend
received a *pneumatique* from Valadon, asking him to come to
the rue Cortot at once. He found her in a terrible state, almost
speechless, her face, neck and arms covered in some gluey material which she was trying to rub off. A gang of bad boys had
waylaid her drunken, overexcited son and rolled him in grease
or oil. He had come home mad with fury, and started to avenge
himself on the *mauvais garçons* by breaking up his mother's fur-

niture. In her efforts to restrain him she had become as filthy as he.

She was still living in the Impasse Guelma when Utrillo was arrested for breaking up a bistro. A messenger came to fetch her in the small hours and she hurried to the police station in the rue Lambert, where things looked exceptionally bad for her son. She paid for the damage and begged that he be saved from prison. Then she took him home—his eyes blackened, his cheeks swollen and his suit torn.

In a lachrymose autobiographical fragment Utrillo described his mother as a saintly woman whom he blessed and venerated. She was a goddess, a sublime creature full of kindness, uprightness, charity, self-sacrifice and devotion, a flower among women. He bitterly regretted that he had not listened to her advice, and he asked his Creator to forgive him.

He was truly sorry whenever he hurt her. Toward others he remained indifferent. He was not a man in need of friendship. In his childhood mother and grandmother had sufficed; at school he was not loved; and by the time he reached manhood he had retired too much into himself to find it easy to get on with other people, especially with his mother's friends. They were intruders who had become between them.

There came a moment when Utter and Valadon could no longer endure Utrillo and the scenes he made. They went to live at 41 rue Saint-Georges, leaving Utrillo in the rue Cortot. But in quite a short time they were back in the studio and communal life started anew with all its ups and downs.

Neither Valadon nor Utter yet realized Utrillo's true importance as a painter of his day. His sense of desolation coupled with his happy blend of colours expressed the feelings of his time with the same force as Verlaine's poetry.

Il pleure dans mon coeur
comme il pleut sur la ville . . .

Utrillo cried in his heart after each bout of drunkenness, and then he painted a street with the cobbles and the walls waiting for the rain.

Louis Vauxcelles was the first art critic to mention him. In the May number of *Gil Blas* in 1912 he praised Utrillo's tumble-down cottages (Montmagny period), his consummate skill as a colourist and his sensibility. "If, one day," he wrote, "a retro-spective exhibition is organized of Montmartre painters from Georges Michel to the present day, Utrillo will have to be included."

In that month of May Utrillo was back in the Sannois nursing home, but Dr. Revertégat gave him comparative liberty. He was allowed to paint out of doors without being annoyed or interrupted. In July the doctor gave him permission to go on a holiday in Brittany with his friend Richmond Chaudois. Libaude wrote at once, exhorting Utrillo not to sell his paintings to anyone else while on holiday and reminding him to deliver six landscapes each month. "I believe we are in complete agreement and I hope we shall remain so for a long time . . ."

Richmond Chaudois was a dear friend of Valadon, Utter and Utrillo—commonly referred to as the trio. He, too, had made his home in the rue Cortot. He was a burly man with round shoulders and a rolling gait, and it was hard to tell whether he was an ex-prizefighter or a keeper of gorillas in an open-air zoo. As a matter of fact, he was a chemist by profession and worked in a laboratory. During the First World War he was to invent a glue used in airplane propellers, and for this he received a pension from the French government. He had a second pension as a disabled ex-service man. The war left him with a huge scar on his cheek which made him look more threatening than ever. He was romantically fond of the underworld and flattered himself that prostitutes, ponces and crooks accepted him as one of themselves. He enjoyed spending his time with them and used to squander his money ostentatiously in their company.

Shortly before the Second World War, a couple of days after he had collected his two quarterly pensions, his body was found in the Seine. The police quickly established that it was not a case of suicide.

When he went to Brittany with Utrillo in the summer of 1912, however, there was no scar on his face and no menace of death. Theirs was a strange but close friendship. One night when Chaudois was drunk on the Butte he raised his voice, shouting, "I am Utrillo, I alone am Utrillo!"

The trio went to Le Conquet where Chaudois had a house. They visited Ouessant during their stay. The island made Utrillo exceptionally nervous. In Le Conquet Valadon was pleased with life. She thought that peace and quiet in wind and hail would do her son good. There was no need to paint from postcards and no reason to fear the bistros, since Utrillo could easily be kept away from them.

Chaudois became Utrillo's porter. Every morning he carried easel, paintbox and canvases to a remote point at some distance from the nearest tavern, and there he guarded Utrillo while he worked. Utrillo produced one painting a day.

Chaudois chatted all the time; Utrillo did not listen; however, when they were ready to leave Utrillo said, "I am tired. Carry me."

Chaudois did not much like the idea. Utrillo was tall, Chaudois short and indolent. None the less he took Utrillo on his back. Utrillo had a simple sense of humour and so he made water down Chaudois' back as he rode on him. For revenge Chaudois filled Utrillo's pockets with pebbles while the painter was working in shirt sleeves. This was to teach him the meaning of weight. When Utrillo had finished painting, he put on his jacket and again forced Chaudois to carry him. So poor Chaudois carried a much heavier Utrillo than before, and happy Utrillo made water on him again.

They stayed for three weeks in Le Conquet. Utrillo painted twenty landscapes. but when they left only nineteen were ac-

counted for. Valadon and Utter were convinced that Utrillo
had bartered the missing picture for a litre or two of wine.
Utrillo hotly denied it. The canvas, he maintained, had disappeared mysteriously. The mystery was not solved until 1950,
when a Breton woman carrying a landscape appeared in Le Vésinet where Utrillo now resided. The landscape was unsigned,
but when Utrillo painted out of doors he did not sign his
pictures until after he got home. It was the missing painting,
now worth a fortune. The original price had been two litres
of red wine.

In the rue Cortot Chaudois lived in a kind of basement, where
the water came in when there was heavy rain. He had a small
stove, and he used to sit beside it, almost scorching himself. Two
decades after the holiday in Brittany a foreign journalist came
to the rue Cortot to get an interview with the famous painter.
Utrillo was out but Chaudois happened to be in the studio. He
passed himself off as Utrillo.

"I, Maurice Utrillo, am the greatest mystic in the world," he
began, then gave the journalist a long, brilliant lecture on different religious sects, inventing them as he went along, on papal
bulls which he also invented on the spur of the moment, and on
his own mystical experiences. The journalist left deeply impressed.

Chaudois accompanied the trio to Genets near Mont Saint-
Michel, where Utrillo was overjoyed and astonished by the strong
alcoholic content of the local cider. It was not the kind of rubbish some of the wine counters sold on the Butte. In the course
of his walks he met M. Georges Aubry, a dilettante picture
dealer, who would not have minded a little artistic chat with
the artist straight from the Butte-Montmartre. That was not
to be, for all he got out of Utrillo was, "But it is unbelievable,
Monsieur Aubry, to find such a degree of alcohol in cider."
They ran into each other every day, and every day M. Aubry saluted him with hope renewed. "But it is unbelievable, Monsieur
Aubry," Utrillo said, "to find such a degree of alcohol in cider."

Chaudois went with the trio when they took their most extensive trip, to Corsica. There Utrillo could not be kept away from the bottle. They stayed in the château of a M. Malespina at Belgodère, forty-three kilometers from Calvi. Utter played cards in the taverns with the muleteers while Utrillo sampled the fierce local *eau de vie*. "Now this is something quite different from the *rhun fantaisie* they sell you in the rue Lepic," he said, smacking his lips. From the château they moved to a hotel.

"He's terrible," Valadon complained. "I wonder what he has under his skin . . . I have seen him doing the lowest things for a litre. Just imagine, I caught him the other night in the hotel, drinking the alcohol from the hot plate."

In Corsica Valadon made the first sketches for her great painting, *Les lanceurs de filets,* now in the Musée National d'Art Moderne in Paris. She painted "complete yet disconcerting landscapes," as Coquiot called them. Utter painted red bridges, calvaries and sharply defined landscapes; and Utrillo lived in the clouds. If he gazed at a landscape his thoughts, he later said, reverted to the streets of the Butte. He did paint the church at the foot of Mont-Cinto. When the painting was finished he peopled the mountainside with a veritable French army, but later he rubbed the soldiers out.

He loved excursions on muleback. One morning he found himself before a stream which the mule firmly refused to cross. Utrillo cajoled, then threatened; however nothing would induce the animal to budge, and nothing would ever induce Utrillo to whip it. He got off the mule and tried to drag it across the stream. In vain. He tried to lift it over. The mule was too heavy. The beast only moved when Utter appeared on the scene and applied the whip Utrillo had refused to use.

Corsica did not inspire him. Years later a woman turned up in the rue Cortot with a painting of the Sacré-Coeur. She came to find out whether Utrillo had painted it. It was not a good painting and she feared that it was a fake. Valadon was ready to agree with the visitor, but when Utrillo saw it he exclaimed,

"I recognize it. Don't you remember? I painted it when we were in Corsica."

The trio and Chaudois spent their last holiday before the Great War in the Forest of Compiègne. Utrillo was at the very height of his talent, painting village churches, white ones, black ones and grey ones. It was his angelic period. *The Small White Church* was painted during that holiday. Beside a white road stands a white church under a white sky. He hardly used any blue for the sky. Most art critics considered the angelic period as his greatest.

Prices for Utrillos were creeping up. They would have gone up quicker if he had not sold paintings so indiscriminately. In 1913 in spite of his arrangement with Libaude he sold paintings to Gay, Marie Vizier, a rag-and-bone man called Delloue and Clovis Sagot among others. The year before, Jourdain had arranged for the Druet Gallery to show six landscapes by Utrillo together with the paintings of Friesz, Manguin, Marquet and Puy. The rue Royale public was not impressed by the work of a Montmartre painter. The Butte was a place to amuse yourself at night, not to look for new talent. The result was similar in the Blot Gallery which Libaude had taken to exhibit Utrillos exclusively. Montmartre landscapes were not yet for the boulevards. "Bistro stuff," was the consensus. Besides, it was well known that you could always get hold of a Utrillo for five francs up on the Butte.

Utrillo's first financial success came in 1914 at the Hôtel Drouot, where four of his paintings were auctioned. *Notre-Dame-de-Paris, La place, Vue de Montmagny* and *Rue de village* fetched, respectively, 400, 270, 130 and 150 francs, sums which neither Utrillo nor his mother expected.

It was not yet plain sailing. On the strength of the sale Libaude put twenty Utrillos up for auction at the Hôtel Drouot. They fetched 576 francs in all. "Not brilliant," Libaude wrote to Utter.

In the spring before the war Utrillo stayed in Dr. Revertégat's

establishment again. Before he left Paris he sold several paintings
to M. Marseille, an art dealer in the rue de Seine.

"It must be obvious to you," Libaude wrote to Utter in
March, "that if on his release from the nursing home he starts
inundating Montmartre with his paintings I shall be unable to
continue my agreement with him."

In April Libaude wrote to Utter again: "I can but confirm
what I have said many times: Maurice Utrillo is a sick man,
probably incurable (several physicians told me so), and one can't
count on the regular production of a sick man, or on his keeping to an agreement. I can't commit myself in any way unless
on leaving the nursing home he puts himself under his mother's
benevolent care. You surely know that he has gone as far as
signing canvases that were not his."

Libaude wrote to Utter once more, insisting on receiving all
Utrillo's work, oils, pastels and water colours, or he could not
go on paying for the nursing home. In June he declared that he
could not continue under the old conditions. He would, he
went on, remain interested in Utrillo if he were given the right
of first refusal. Utter turned that down. Libaude's next offer
was to buy four paintings a month, but without entering into
any formal agreement. That offer was turned down too. On
July 12 he wrote to Utter saying Utrillo could go his own way.
Thus ended a business relationship that had lasted for five years.

2

One night in July 1914 Utrillo rushed into La Belle Gabrielle with the evening paper, shouting that the Kaiser had refused to accept England's offer of mediation. He was the first
with the news, and even Depaquit could not think up a joke
when he heard it. Then came August 1 and general mobiliza-
tion. Montmartre emptied, for most of the artists and writers
were of military age.

Utter was called up. Though both had already engaged in

little affairs on the side, Valadon and Utter were still in love. Their first reaction to war and Utter's imminent departure was to get married, at the Mairie of the 18th *arrondissement* on September 1. Then Utter went to the war, was wounded and spent the rest of it in the quartermaster's store near Lyons.

Utrillo did not have his medical examination until May 1915. It took place in Argenton and the once robust fellow was found unfit for service.

"He was so dejected," said Jean Dufy, the painter, when speaking of the Butte during the First World War, "that he painted the cathedral of Rheims in flames, the cathedral, naturally, from a postcard, the flames from his imagination." As part of his war effort Utrillo also painted a picture of the Kaiser, a punchinello with a grotesque moustache, riding in a hearse.

Utrillo fell back on Gay, Delloue, rag-and-bone men and bistros, and his favourite tavern Au Vieux Montmartre, previously known as Le Petit Trou, in the rue d'Ursel. Charles Besson, the proprietor, served food and drink to painters who, in the best Utrillo tradition, paid their bills with canvases. Besson first bought Utrillos from Gay; later he took them direct from the artist.

Utrillo's wartime production amounted to about twelve hundred paintings. The number does not include drawings and water colours. He went about with his hands, jacket and trousers covered in paint. "One just couldn't believe that he ever worked," a Montmartre publican once observed. "He was always in bistros."

He used to fill his pockets with miniature bottles of absinthe and liqueurs which were given away as samples. He drank their contents during his morning strolls. If he had money he drank sparkling wine with a plate of kidneys, his favourite dish. In the afternoon he returned either to Valadon if she was in residence in the rue Cortot or to the Casse-Croûte if she was visiting her soldier-husband.

His daytime strolls did him no harm. In the afternoons he

painted from postcards. But when night enveloped Montmartre, there was no holding him. At his wit's end Gay locked him in, but that did not restrain Utrillo. Thirst made him as agile as a monkey. He jumped out through the window, landing on the steps of the rue Mont-Cenis, and made for the first bistro. His nights out often ended at the police station.

In 1915 his mother put him into the nursing home of Dr. Laforêt near Lyons. The doctor observed with horror that Utrillo could absorb from eight to ten litres of wine a day. The doctor had already heard from Gay that Utrillo had drunk five bottles of Mme. Gay's wartime reserve of eau de Cologne and a bottle of varnish.

His creative spirit, noted Carco, was dependent on the quantity of wine he consumed. But Carco forgot, or, because he did not want to spoil the story, did not bother to add that even Utrillo could reach a stage where drink interfered with his work. Yet when he was in a nursing home, where drink was kept from him, he painted equally well. There he accepted the rules; in the outside world he rejected them.

Madeleine died in 1915. The trio—Utter was on leave—went to bury her in the cemetery of Saint-Ouen. "Grandmother never quite appreciated her unique role in the history of painting," Valadon said to Creixams. That, of course, is a moot point.

In the following year while Valadon was away at Lyons, Utrillo was shut up in the mental hospital of Villejuif on his doctor's advice. He was put in the ward for male lunatics, some of them raving. Villejuif was the result of too many and too noisy scandals: his nerves were in a bad way; and since he had never practiced self-control his behaviour was considered dangerously violent. The police might have taken more drastic action. Still, there was no valid reason, his friends believed, to lock him up in the company of maniacs. After all, drink was his only trouble. In a letter to Gay, Utrillo said, "I was sent to Villejuif not as mentally sick but because of the bad state of my nerves caused by public suffering."

"Life is no fun here," he wrote in another letter, "but one must submit to it and one has to be reasonable in this sick milieu. You, who are privileged to remain on the picturesque Butte, must tell me what is going on. What is happening? What is the latest gossip in the neighbourhood? Have you seen Tiret-Bognet, that dear companion with undeniable talent? Ah, Montmartre with its provincial corners and bohemian habits! One ought to write stories about the district which is so original and independent. It is regrettable that the sad occurrences that brought me here ever took place. I would be so at my ease beside you, installed in your room, composing a motif with a road and houses painted with whitewash. Or something different altogether."

According to Utter, Utrillo attached immense importance to his different periods in nursing homes, considering them an essential part of life, which, in fact, nursing homes had become for him. He could not imagine anyone going through life without spending some time in such establishments. It was, so to speak, a procedure every normal person should follow. He admitted that he was an alcoholic, but for him it was an illness like mumps or scarlet fever. He spoke of his time in nursing homes as one speaks of holidays. Villejuif, however, was a different matter; you could not develop a holiday spirit there.

When they allowed him to go he was discharged only conditionally. In short, he had been warned. None the less he dropped back into the ditch of drunkenness shortly after his return to the Casse-Croûte. This time he stayed in the asylum from August to November, long enough to make him think. Yet in 1917 he was to be locked up again, in the mental hospital of Picpus, still as a voluntary patient.

His mother spent as much time as she could with her soldiering husband. But that did not stop her from carrying on a love affair with Erik Satie, the composer, when she was in Paris. During one of their tiffs she so angered Satie that the gentle, timid composer pushed her out through the ground-floor window of his flat. She fell on the pavement, and in his fright

Satie ran to the police station, shouting: "I've killed her." He returned with the policemen to the scene of his crime. Nobody was there, for Valadon, entirely unhurt, had strolled home in the meanwhile. "Reminded me of my circus days," she said. The following day she rejoined Utter at Belleville-sur-Saône. He was still a private in the 158th Infantry Regiment.

Utrillo wrote to her, assuring her that his will power was of steel. He spoke of some woman called Marie whom he branded as an enemy. He had done a painting for M. Firmin, a police sergeant, whom he thought a nice chap. "André Utter," he went on, "is a decent fellow whom I envy. Your place is in the Louvre, mine in a nursing home. I am aware of that. I ruined my life at the age of sixteen, and it is too late to find myself a niche in this bourgeois world." She could ask him anything she wanted, and she would find not only a son but also a slave. However, the devil of alcohol tyrannized him. He ended his letter with warm greetings to Utter.

During 1917, Utrillo lived mostly with Gay. "I'll always welcome you, any time, any hour, whatever state you are in," Gay had written while he was in Villejuif. Gay was now a busy man as he had a second shop in the rue Rochechouart. In the morning he sold beef and chicken, in the afternoon paintings, including Utrillos. Twenty francs was the highest price he asked for a picture.

"Why do you sell such good stuff in the morning and such rubbish in the afternoon?" asked a waggish client.

Utrillo met Zborowski, the dealer who played such an important and benevolent part in Modigliani's career, and sold him a few paintings. His favourite dealer at the time was Delloue in the rue de Clignancourt, yet he ranged as far as the rue Victor-Massé, where at Number 25, Berthe Weill had her shop. She had begun with antiques and old prints; paintings came afterward. Steinlen, Forain and Willette were the first modern artists whose work she sold. Daumier and Lautrec were in least demand. She was the first dealer to sell Picasso's work in Paris.

She bought three paintings, a bull-fight sequence, for a hundred francs and then sold it for a hundred and fifty. She said it was she who had introduced Max Jacob to Picasso; Jacob said they had met in the Lapin Agile.

She had already exhibited Valadon's and Utter's work in 1913 together with paintings by Charmy, Levitzka, Lacost, Lhote and Ribemont-Dessaignes. She called them her second best. The show was a complete failure.

One day in 1917 Utrillo appeared in the rue Victor-Massé with a painting on cardboard. He called it *Effect of Snow*, and asked ten francs for it. She hesitated, though not because she was aware that his paintings fetched more in the sale room, but because she found him so overexcited. None the less she bought *Effect of Snow* for ten francs. Next day he returned even more overexcited, offering another painting. "Only a hundred sous," he pleaded, but this time in vain.

Her troubles were not over. Modigliani came a few days later. He was in a fine state too, falling all over the place. She was petrified that he might collapse on her. She sent him packing. It was a shame, she sighed, for such a civilized and cultured person to be such a drunk.

According to their friend Henri-Georges Cheval, a painter, Modigliani had come to Berthe Weill so soon after Utrillo's visits because the two friends were in constant communication about dealers. If one found a dealer who exchanged his work against drinking money without fuss he immediately informed the other.

In the same year, while he was on leave, Utter arranged with Berthe Weill to show his and Valadon's paintings. Utter knew how to persuade dealers. The exhibition was well frequented but only a few pictures were sold. Berthe Weill was even less lucky with Modigliani. On the varnishing day of his show the police commissioner of the district ordered the nudes to be taken down. The exhibition had to be closed.

One thinks of the 1914–18 war as carnage succeeding carnage

and nothing else, yet in the art world business was flourishing. Even that weighty art critic Gustave Coquiot embarked on buying and selling paintings. Berthe Weill, who was no critic but only a dealer, rather resented that. "Business is good," she wrote. "This war has produced its own anomalies." Coquiot used his flat as his business premises. It was well stocked with paintings, and patrons of art were exceedingly well received and given cigars, port and choice liqueurs.

"Coquiot," Berthe Weill went on, "shows them the paintings without really showing them. '*Tenez*,' he says, 'I bought this from a poor creature who was starving to death. . . .' "

Those words, she maintained, were repeated daily in the dense cigar smoke. Coquiot possessed several paintings of his friends Valadon, Utrillo and Utter. Now they were for sale too, and, needless to say, Valadon had many quarrels with the friend turned dealer.

"I sheltered her," Coquiot complained to Weill.

"He's eaten me out of house and home," Valadon accused.

It was all great fun, but when in 1918 Big Bertha lobbed its shells into Paris, Berthe closed her gallery and scurried off to La Baule.

3

Among Montmartre's profane martyrs were Gérard de Nerval, André Gill and Lautrec; however, they had belonged to the last century. In this century Amedeo Modigliani was their worthy successor. He had lived in Montparnasse towards the end of his life; still, he had been a long time in Montmartre. When he arrived from Italy he was an elegant dandy, but alcohol and hashish took their toll. His features coarsened, he no longer rode in fiacres but dragged himself along wearily, dressed in brown velvet like any Piedmontese peasant, a red scarf round his neck. He carried a folder containing drawings under his arm, selling them for a little cash, or tearing them up in anger or despair.

In the rue Norvins lived an Englishwoman, Beatrice Hastings, who had been his mistress. She was a nervous woman who was afraid of burglars and also of her temperamental ex-lover. She had armed herself with a pistol. Modigliani knew that, and whenever he was fighting drunk and found himself in the vicinity, he burst in on her and they exchanged pistol shots. Neither of them came to any harm. Still, her fear increased and out of sheer charity Max Jacob spent many nights in her flat to safeguard her from burglars and Modigliani.

Modigliani had faithful friends, Carco and Dr. Alexandre among them, and Zborowski, his friend and dealer, who never abandoned him. He became insufferable when he was drunk. Whereas Utrillo's fights were forced upon him, Modigliani sought them out. He often got mixed up in brawls over prostitutes in the Place Clichy, though his usual drinking quarters were in the Boulevard du Montparnasse. "Queer," Picasso observed. "You may find Utrillo drunk anywhere, at the Bourse or Place d'Italie, but Modigliani is always drunk right in front of the Coupole or the Dôme."

In a Left Bank café a good forty years after Modigliani's death, Robert Giraud, the author of *Le vin des rues,* ran into one of Modigliani's surviving cronies. "Tell me everything you remember about him," said Giraud.

The crony thought for a long time. "He still owes me five francs," he said at last.

Legend has it that when Utrillo and Modigliani met for the first time they fell rapturously into each other's arms, then nearly came to blows because each maintained that the other was the greater painter of the two.

Mme. Fernande Barrey, who had often sat with them in Montparnasse cafés, said Modigliani was a brilliant talker; Utrillo was not. When asked what opinion she had formed of their friendship, she answered, "They were two comedians. They played up to each other but were not really fond of each other."

During a visit Utrillo paid to Montparnasse he went with

Mme. Barrey and Modigliani to a café near the cemetery. A funeral procession came along and Utrillo made the sign of the Cross. He crossed himself again when the second hearse appeared; when the third came he showed signs of nervousness; and on the arrival of the fourth he exclaimed as he crossed himself yet again, "The dead make me sick."

"Utrillo was less afraid of people than of having his drink taken from him," observed Mme. Barrey.

Henri-Georges Cheval witnessed a scene one night between the two friends. Utrillo had been making a lot of noise when suddenly Modigliani turned on him, "Shut up, you grandson of a washerwoman."

Whether they were comedians or not, the two painters were constantly in each other's company and when they were apart, something always seemed to bring them together. One night Modigliani found Utrillo drunk in a small bistro. Though he himself had been drinking heavily too, Modigliani managed to take Utrillo back to his studio for the night, and in the morning he accompanied him to the rue Cortot.

Valadon, said Modigliani, was the only woman who understood him. She was fond of him. "He was a beautiful being," she said, "fine, sensitive, also something of a joker."

Late one night he burst into the studio in the rue Cortot. He brought a bottle with him; his features were haggard, his voice slurred.

"Have you a glass, Valadon?" Modigliani asked.

"You don't need one," Valadon replied.

"Do you want me to drink from the bottle?"

"You aren't thirsty any more. Come along, I'll take you home."

He was lodging in the rue Norvins. Valadon practically carried him through the deserted streets. He sang lustily. They found Utrillo in Modigliani's room. He looked like a blackamoor, for the paraffin lamp was smoking and he had wiped his face with his sooty hand. They had a good laugh. Valadon

wanted to take her son home as they all needed a good rest.
"Not before we thank the Lord," Utrillo said. She thought
that could wait until the morning. "Right now," insisted
Utrillo.

Utrillo and Modigliani fell on their knees and sang the
Kyrie eleison, the Gloria and the Sanctus.

Another day Utrillo turned up in Rosalie's bistro-restaurant
in the rue Campagne-Première. Rosalie hailed from Leghorn like
Modigliani, who took most of his meals in her establishment.
Utrillo was in socks and he could not recollect where he had
left his shoes. He asked Rosalie to send for pastels, and when
they arrived he sketched the Lapin Agile on the wall. Apparently,
his experience with Marie Vizier had taught him nothing.
Modigliani entered and the two friends celebrated their chance
meeting. They had soon spent all their money, but Rosalie refused to give them credit. A terrible altercation ensued with
Rosalie and Modigliani swearing in Italian, Utrillo keeping them
company in French. Passers-by stopped to listen. Utrillo had
a sudden brainwave: Rosalie should pay them for his sketch
on the wall. Rosalie refused, shrieking, "I can't cut my wall
to pieces to pay my wine merchant." Her words made the two
painters even angrier, and, as happens if one is heavy with drink
and indignation, Modigliani remembered that Utrillo had
never returned a pair of trousers he had lent him.

"When you give me back the coat I have lent you!" retorted
Utrillo, and they started to fight. They made such a din that
the police came and they were taken to the station, where,
luckily, Utrillo remembered the name of an official at the Pré-
fecture de Police who was a friend of artists. They were set
free. Though still drunk they were friends again.

On another occasion soon after Utrillo's discharge from Picpus
he had gone to Montparnasse and Modigliani put him up for
the night. Utrillo was the first to awake in the morning. He
purloined Modigliani's overcoat and tiptoed out of the house.
When Modigliani opened his eyes and saw that his overcoat and

his friend were missing he rushed to Zborowski, who went in search of Utrillo. He found him not far from the house where he had spent the night, arguing with an old-clothesman to whom he was trying to sell not only the overcoat but also some of his own garments. Zborowski dragged him away, Modigliani took back his overcoat, and the friends were friends again.

On another night Modigliani turned up in the rue Cortot with a bottle of brandy. It was raining cats and dogs and Modigliani was wet to the skin. "Where is Maurice?" he asked. Valadon said her son was in bed. Modigliani wanted to wake him up because, he declared, Utrillo was the only person who appreciated him. Valadon barred his passage. Modigliani sat down, announcing, "We'll have a drink." Valadon did not want one, so he invited Utter to drink with him. Utter accepted a little brandy. Modigliani filled half a glass for himself.

"You'd better take off your wet things and sleep on the sofa in the studio," Valadon suggested.

Modigliani rose, picked up the bottle and without glancing at either of them stalked out of the house.

When Modigliani visited the Butte he often went in Utrillo's company to La Belle Gabrielle, where they drank with Père la Butte, a drunken, bearded old news vendor whom they plied with drink, nobody bothering about payment. "All they needed was Père la Butte," was Marie Vizier's comment.

There used to be on the Butte a lean-faced man who considered himself an art dealer. His office was the café he daily visited, his shop the banquette on which he always kept a few unframed pictures which, to the café keeper's annoyance, he showed to anyone who looked like a possible customer. He had faith in his judgement. "This is a Friesz," he would say, showing a small canvas. It was not. "This is an Isabey." It was nothing of the sort. "Ah, but this one is an early Renoir." It was a poor daub.

He was once offered a Utrillo. He refused to buy it though it went dirt-cheap. It was a Sacré-Coeur and looked like the genuine article. He thought it was not a Utrillo but some stupid joke. It was signed by Modigliani, signed six times at least, signed all round the canvas.

That picture might have made the fortune of the poor man.

One can almost see Utrillo finishing the painting, then asking his dear friend to sign it for a lark, and laughing loudly as the two friends sallied forth arm in arm, making for the rue Campagne-Première.

The number of stories about the two friends' drunken outings is legion. One is left with the impression that neither of them did anything else. Yet they were both at the height of their talents and working hard.

Utrillo was no longer satisfied with the original five colours. The decision to add exuberant colours had come to him in Villejuif. Tabarant called it "truculent colouring." His painting of the church of Villejuif looked as though the church had been set on fire. He now used seven colours. It was his fourth period. Much later he was to add a green and a luminous orange to his palette.

And while the friends drank and painted the war came to an end. Among the *habitués* of the Lapin Agile, Guillaume Apollinaire was the first victim of the approaching peace. The soldier poet had survived the great slaughter only to be carried off by Spanish flu.

> *Le vent vient du couchant*
> *Le métal des caroubiers*
>
> *Tout est plus triste qu'autrefois*
> *Tous les dieux terrestres vieillissent*
> *L'univers se plaint par ta voix*
> *Et des êtres nouveaux surgissent*
> *Trois par trois*

As he lay dying the happy people, released from fear and nightmare, shouted under his window, "*À bas Guillaume!*" meaning, of course, the Kaiser.

Apollinaire died on November 9 and was buried on Armistice Day. Church bells rang, salvos were fired, gay crowds thronged the streets, and the hearse was accompanied by a detachment of the 225 Territorial Regiment. It passed under triumphal arches and there were flags and bunting everywhere.

Modigliani's turn came in 1920. He died of tuberculosis in La Charité Hospital. He left behind poor Jeanne Hébuterne, a gentle girl whom his friends had liked, for they had hoped that she would be the saving of him. But she loved him so much that she accepted whatever he did as wonderful and perfect. She put up with anything for his sake. Manolo Ortiz de Zárate found them once on a paillasse, covered in olive oil, surrounded by empty sardine tins.

"*Cara, cara Italia,*" were Modigliani's last words.

"Bury him like a prince," cabled his brother, who was Socialist Deputy for Leghorn. Modigliani was given a sumptuous funeral, and his friends could not help laughing when his old enemies the policemen saluted as the hearse trundled past.

Valadon was present at the funeral, a big affair with flowers and wreaths galore. They were piled high on the hearse and they shook and danced with every step the horses took. The shaking and dancing reminded Valadon of Modigliani's gait when he was drunk.

"But the flowers!" Valadon laughed as she thought of the florists who would never get their money.

Jeanne Hébuterne did not laugh. She threw herself from a window of her parents' house near Père Lachaise. She had returned to live with them when Modigliani was taken to hospital. She was three months pregnant.

Utrillo did not return to Montparnasse after his friend's death.

The Mishap
and the Château

1

CARCO visited Utrillo in the mental hospital of Picpus during his second voluntary confinement. Picpus is a dreary neighbourhood with hospitals, cemeteries and old people's homes, not far from the Place de la Nation. Carco found him in a private cell, with a window giving on the courtyard. Utrillo complained of the noise the lunatics made in the public ward. He was completely lucid, and the doctors considered him a quiet patient who would soon be released. Carco had smuggled in half a bottle of champagne. Utrillo did not grab it but contemplated it sadly. Then he hid it under the blanket. Deeply moved, Carco departed only to hear a few days later that Utrillo had escaped.

Utrillo was twice a voluntary patient at Picpus between the late autumn of 1918 and the spring of 1919. A voluntary patient was not treated with the same severity as the certified insane. But suddenly Dr. Briand, who was in charge of the lunatic asylums of the department of the Seine, discovered in his files that one Maurice Utrillo had been discharged only conditionally from Villejuif in 1916, yet the man was in one of his mental hospitals again as a voluntary patient. That would not do. He pronounced Utrillo officially insane, and put him into the public ward.

Valadon came running, clamouring for her son. She was not received cordially; her entreaties were in vain, and Utrillo was kept in Picpus for nearly a year. He had a number like all the detained mental patients.

In order to make life easier for him Valadon insisted on his remaining a paying patient, although she had no means. The 720 francs a month was too large a sum for Zborowski, who had stepped into Libaude's shoes. However, one of his clients, M. Necker, came to the rescue. He was an admirer of both Utrillo's and Modigliani's work, and possessed about one hundred examples of their work. M. Necker agreed to pay half of the monthly sum. Zborowski paid the other half. By the autumn of 1919, however, Zborowski had to withdraw because he could no longer afford to pay his share in spite of the five or six paintings he received monthly from Utrillo. Chaudois stepped in, persuading a manufacturer friend of his to hang a Utrillo in every room of his freshly decorated house.

Utrillo continued to paint in the hospital. The male nurses responsible for taking care of him stole some of his paintings. They became afraid that they might be discovered and decided to get rid of Utrillo. They gave him a little money, filled him with drink, and when night fell, took him into the garden where he easily escaped. He hurried home to the rue Cortot, where he fell into his mother's arms.

The consequences were not as unpleasant as might have been expected. The authorities at Picpus only insisted that Valadon keep a male nurse to look after her son. They probably feared a scandal if the story of the stolen pictures became public knowledge. They themselves provided Utrillo with the nurse. He was a Breton called Pierre, a big, hefty fellow whom Utrillo often gave the slip. Pierre was a religious man, and Utrillo's friends said he crossed himself whenever he looked at his patient's pictures of churches. He did not last long, and when he left Utrillo became a free agent again in every way.

Utrillo had had several warnings; he had been confined among raving lunatics and Picpus was no bucolic retreat. None the less he returned to his old way of life. His manners in public became even worse. He had taken to exposing himself. An old lady, a friend of Modigliani, still remembers several occasions when, while sitting beside her in a Montparnasse café, he suddenly exposed himself.

"It's my head," he said, when she remonstrated with him.

At other times he shouted: "I paint with it."

The Butte was accustomed to him and his ways. The policemen either gave him a beating or made him paint for them. Women ran from him, but that was not a serious matter; men laughed or hit him. His reputation was rapidly growing and the price of his work rose with it, one more reason to be tolerant with him. In any case, the Butte was a village, and though villagers like to wash their dirty linen in public, they do not take it to be washed elsewhere. Utrillo was safe while he remained on the hillock, and Valadon and Utter were always there to protect and save him.

But the day came when he threw caution to the wind. He had been drinking so heavily that for once he overreached himself. He closed his umbrella, as it were, while it was raining hard.

It was June 1921. He was blind drunk and had no idea where he was going, for if he had, he wouldn't have strayed from Montmartre. He roared down into Paris, shouting and gesticulating, and reached the Place de la Bourse, alien soil to him. He went into the public lavatory and emerged with his trousers down. He had already attracted the attention of a couple of policemen with his shouting. Now they fell on him. Drunk as he was, he could still remember that policemen were no well-wishers of his and he tried to defend himself.

Under a hail of kicks, he was dragged to the police station. The commissioner was a stranger who had never heard of Litrillo. He was taken to the Tribunal de flagrants délits, a magistrate's court, accused of drunkenness and immoral behaviour. The police dropped the last charge but added resisting arrest. Utrillo was sent to the Santé Prison. His two cell mates were pickpockets.

Valadon arrived. "Is that your son?" the warder asked. She said he was. "Congratulations," said the warder.

On June 24 Utrillo wrote to Berthe Weill: "From the Santé, 2nd Division, Judge Delalé . . . I was happy to hear that the exhibition of my work was successful and that you sold a number of paintings. I deeply regret having been unable to visit the exhibition as there were also shown some of my mother's paintings, and it always gives me great joy to see and see again the admirable pictures she paints with such genius. She is a great artist and she paints marvellously."

On June 29 he wrote to Gay: "I am released from all further persecution—I am suffering from all sorts of vexations—I have no idea what the omnipotent authorities intend to do with me. I am very impatient to be liberated at last. I want to be free in order to work and behave reasonably."

The brutal behaviour of the police on the day of his arrest became known, and letters of protest against the treatment he had received were published in the newspapers. The public attorney ordered a medical examination. He should have done so in the first place. The police doctor decided to release Utrillo from prison and send him to a lunatic asylum. He was allowed to take painting materials with him. He was put into Sainte-Anne but remained there only for eight days. Then he was transferred to Dr. Delmas' establishment in the Place de la Mairie at Ivry.

On July 9 he wrote to Gay: "Thank you very much for the interest you take in my sad situation due to drink . . . There

exist baneful influences in life which have their repercussions
on health, liberty and now and then on the talent of those
who succumb to them."

So far so good. He was in the state of remorse which often
followed his fits of drinking. He was no longer in prison, he
was allowed to paint, the tiresome business would soon blow
over and then he could start from scratch again. He did not
know that he had been confined to the asylum for good, and
that the authorities had no intention of restoring him to liberty.
But Valadon knew, and she persuaded Vallette, the director of
Mercure de France and his wife, Rachilde, the actress, to in-
tervene on her son's behalf. The authorities freed Utrillo on
the condition that he stayed under the care of his mother and
a male nurse, never again to go out alone. If he did so he would
be locked up for life.

Now and then Utrillo managed to escape from mother or
male nurse, but his liberty was always short-lived. The fear
of being confined for life in a lunatic asylum accompanied
him during his brief forays—he dared not to stray far. If he
went to the Lapin Agile or the Place du Tertre his mother
was immediately informed, and then either she or Utter or the
nurse would go to fetch him home.

Gone were the days when he roamed the Butte at will, running
from bistro to bistro, drinking to his heart's content before
collapsing into a hospitable gutter. The streets he had immortalized seldom saw him unaccompanied. He had miscalculated on
that June afternoon. Up on the Butte it could not have happened. He resented that incident for the rest of his life. He
felt about it rather like one who had been crippled in a car
accident as a result of another's bad driving. With the escapade
in the Place de la Bourse, Utrillo had lost what he most cherished. And he was to live another thirty-four years in the
shadow of perpetual confinement.

Utrillo was now a certified lunatic who, if not for his talent,
would have eked out his existence in an asylum. After his first

spell in Sainte-Anne Dr. Ettlinger had told Valadon there were no signs of dementia, but his behaviour was infantile. The creators of his legend frequently quoted Baudelaire's dictum: *"Le génie n'est que l'enfance retrouvée,"* and they compared him to Dostoievski's Prince Myshkin, Edgar Allan Poe and even to the Prince of Denmark. On the other hand, those who were more interested in the man than in the legend did not consider him insane. He had no manners, no discipline, and he was neurotic; but he behaved like a madman only when it suited him. It depended on the circumstances; if he thought it was to his advantage, he behaved normally. He could be cunning and circumspect. He slipped up only once, but that was due to drink, not madness.

He had been spoilt. He always had his way with his mother and grandmother, and since his wants were few and easily satisfied, he saw no reason to conform. He exaggerated his childishness because he found no opposition at home and because it was a safe means of escape. He lost his temper and smashed glasses and furniture because he was immature.

He was without culture. He never visited a museum, and next to his mother and Tiret-Bognet he admired only the paintings of Jean-François Raffaëlli, who painted barracks, fortifications and suburban streets. He read and understood little that was not of momentary interest. He was romantic in the sense that a schoolboy is romantic. He wanted to paint Joan of Arc brandishing her sword, unfurling her banner. He often confused history with religion. He wrote bad poetry and was proud of himself because he could blow a trumpet. In short, he remained an immature person all his life. But his immaturity was balanced by his genius. It made him paint streets and squares and not the Maid of Orleans.

He was not completely at fault. Those around him encouraged his childishness. His mother and stepfather gave him toys to play with, and the sycophants applauded his stupidest remarks. "Let him do whatever he fancies as long as it keeps him quiet," was the general attitude toward him, the same attitude his grandmother held when Utrillo was a schoolboy. Had he not been an alcoholic he would probably have been a humble, apologetic person. And it cannot be sufficiently emphasized that he had no more sense of shame than a small child urinating in the street.

"He was a simple person who felt embarrassed in other people's company," M. Gilbert Gruet of the Bernheim-Jeune Gallery said of him. "He played the idiot because he wanted to be left alone."

"One couldn't get under his skin," said Paulo Gérard of the Lapin Agile. "He was a fugitive, a phantom, an impossible drunk. He liked to drink alone, preferring a dark corner. He vanished if anyone entered. He was a boneless man. He gave you the impression that you could fold him like a folding chair. But he was intelligent. He either shuffled or ran."

Jean Vertex, the writer, thought that Utrillo was more neurotic than mad. In a different milieu and without his art he would have ended his days either in prison or in a mental home.

He could be immensely kind and friendly. Once Vertex ran into him on the Butte. Utrillo had just finished two paintings of the Moulin de la Galette. "I haven't a centime," he said. "I can't buy a drink."

"Come with me," said Vertex, and they went to Birbaum's *épicerie-buvette*, where they drank two litres of wine, at thirty-five centimes a litre. Vertex paid with a five-franc note. "Keep the change," he said to Utrillo.

Utrillo made him a present of the two canvases. "These are yours," he said. "You've given me pleasure."

Generally, Berthe Weill was critical of Utrillo's behaviour; and she was not given to fulsome praise. Yet when she had spent a Christmas in the rue Cortot, where the buffet was sumptuous and the singing and dancing lasted until morning, she noted in her diary that Utrillo was very gay and did not drink too much. "He was simply marvellous."

Utrillo was present at a dinner given by a famous physician in his house at Verneuil. He took little notice of his surroundings but came alive when the physician was speaking of his medical career. So he was a doctor, and doctors meant mental hospitals. Utrillo began to shriek, pulled the cloth off the table, and threw plates and cutlery at host and guests until he was restrained and led away. "I am mad when it suits me," he observed afterward.

When Utrillo was no longer allowed out alone Valadon and Utter relied on their various friends to accompany him on his walks. This was known as *promener Maurice*. Coquiot took him out frequently in the early twenties. They talked of many things.

Utrillo spoke as though he were a diligent reader. He read, he said, Edgar Allan Poe, *The Tales of Hoffmann* and adventure stories like the novels of Gustave Aimard, Fenimore Cooper and Jean Hire. His favourite was Victor Hugo, though he had time to read only a few of his books. He modestly admitted that he was a writer too.

"What do you like writing?" Coquiot asked.

"Pamphlets against injustice and scandal mongering, and poems full of tenderness, exalting virtue and purity."

Utrillo then showed his writings, bits of crumpled paper, each word written in a different colour.

Utrillo said he was fond of Goethe's *Faust*, especially the second part. (That must have surprised Coquiot.) Goethe wanted to symbolize Nature. He said he could not make out why he was fond of Goethe since he, Utrillo, was not interested in painting male figures (though, he modestly admitted, he painted male figures reasonably well, but the farther away they were on his canvases the more pleased he was). He attached more importance to women than to men. He gave his women large hips and fat buttocks. "I see them," he said, "as laying hens." He did not paint portraits because he was too timid. He had never painted a still life though inanimate objects like fruit and flowers did not give him a sense of malaise. It was different with animals, especially with cats. He feared being alone with a cat because all of a sudden it would follow something invisible.

Utrillo was full of curious ideas, but timidity handicapped him in argument. The same timidity held him aloof from people. Even as a young man he had been reluctant to accompany his friends to the Bal du Moulin de la Galette, because he was afraid of being jostled or having to enter into conversation with someone. Women frightened him more than men. Also the noise and the dancing worried him. "Isn't my overcoat too loud?" he would ask. It was black.

Whereas Renoir had painted the Moulin de la Galette from the inside, Utrillo painted it only from the outside. The joys of young people dancing and laughing and kissing did not inspire him. He preferred drinking alone at home, for bistros were not as private as one's own bedroom.

"Why are others allowed to get drunk but not I?" Utrillo often asked.

"Because others are quiet when they get drunk," Coquiot replied.

In the rue Cortot Utrillo's bedroom-cum-studio was as small and severe as a cell. He brought Coquiot to his room because he wanted the art critic to hear him play the piano. The piano in question was a toy piano, bought in the children's department of a big store. None the less Utrillo took his one-finger playing as seriously as though he were a concert pianist. "It sounds like knocking against porcelain," he observed, trying to find the right note.

The servant brought in a harmonium which Valadon had just purchased for him. "At last I'll be able to play tunes," Utrillo cried. Vigorously he attacked the harmonium. "I mustn't make too much noise," he added. "A poet lives below me and he becomes annoyed when I interfere with his rhymes. What a shame that we can't stand one another."

M. Reverdy, the poet, had fired a pistol shot through the ceiling, so angered was he at Utrillo's rampaging.

Utrillo tried to play *Le quadrille de Madame Angot* on the harmonium. Later, with both feet on the pedals, he attempted *La marche de Sambre et Meuse.* "What will M. Reverdy say?" Coquiot asked, but enthusiasm had got the better of Utrillo. When he could not find the right note he sang it. Eventually he lost his temper and made a fearful racket, banging the harmonium while he kept his feet on the pedals.

Utrillo's favourite idea, of which he often spoke, was that painters should be given ranks like soldiers.

"One does that all the time, dear Maurice," laughed Coquiot.

"Oh I know, but what I mean is stripes on the sleeves. Then people in the street would know exactly who one was. What would my rank be in your opinion? Sergeant?"

"Marshal of France," replied the art critic, who was doing exceedingly well out of Utrillo's paintings.

They dined together at the Clairon de Sébastopol in the Place du Tertre. The inn sign fascinated Utrillo. "So he was a bugler at Sébastopol?" asked Utrillo, pointing to the inn keeper.

"He or someone else, it doesn't really matter," said Coquiot soothingly. Utrillo was pretty high by then.

"Is it a great thing to be a bugler?"

"Easier than being a good painter."

"I'll ask *maman* to buy me a bugle and then I'll come here and blow it."

"And you'll get into trouble again."

Utrillo lapsed into dark silence. Why were others allowed to blow bugles and not he?

One night Pedro Creixams took Utrillo to a restaurant in Low Montmartre which was renowned for its *boeuf à la mode.* Utrillo had wanted to go there for a long time. "So we'll eat *boeuf à la mode,*" Utrillo said a dozen times at least, as they walked to the restaurant. "So this is where we'll eat *boeuf à la mode,*" he said when they reached the restaurant. Creixams ordered *boeuf à la mode.* "Is this it?" Utrillo asked anxiously when the dish arrived. Creixams assured him that it was. "Wonderful," said Utrillo every few seconds. "This is real *boeuf à la mode.* The best I've ever eaten. Wonderful, wonderful!"

"He hardly touched it," Creixams observed.

One late afternoon Alfred Bar was in his flat in the Avenue Junot. The bell rang: Utrillo was at the door. Though he knew that the trio had moved to the Avenue Junot, Bar was surprised to see the painter, who had never called on him before. Bar's flat was a small one of two rooms, the walls of both rooms lined with books. He offered Utrillo a glass of wine, then asked what brought him there.

"I haven't seen you for a long time," said Utrillo.

"About ten years," said Bar.

"But now that we both live here I want to see a lot of you."

Bar said he was always pleased to see him, gave him more wine, time dragged on and Bar had to meet an appointment on the Butte. "I have to go out," he said. Utrillo begged him to let him stay. There were so many interesting books on the shelves and he had so seldom the chance to read, so could he just sit there quietly and read? Bar agreed. Anyway, he was coming back in an hour's time.

Bar's appointment was at La Mère Catherine. Suddenly Utter appeared, panting. "I looked into every bistro on the Butte," he said, "but I can't find Maurice. He's given us the slip. Where can he be?"

"In my flat," Bar said.

"Then let's go at once to your flat," said Utter. "He is not allowed out alone."

Bar had been abroad for several years, so he had not heard of the incident in the Place de la Bourse and its consequences. They went back to the flat: there was no sign of Utrillo.

"See how cunning he is?" said Utter. "He knew I'd be searching the neighbourhood for him, so he came here and waited till he thought I must have finished looking for him on the

Butte and gone on to Low Montmartre. As soon as he thought
the road was clear he left for one of the local bistros, believing
that I wouldn't go back to it."

"You ought to have seen how charmingly he behaved when
he arrived in my flat," Bar remembered. "He really made me
believe that he had come to see me purely for the pleasure of
my company."

In short, his friends and companions considered him childlike, cunning, a liar, a taciturn fellow capable of making a lot
of noise, but they never felt the fear or repugnance, or even
pity a lunatic is wont to inspire. Perhaps the friend who came
to understand him best was Robert Naly, the painter who graduated to painting through the Bourse. He was a stockbroker
before turning to painting and etching. Thus he came to the
Butte from a very different world, which was one of the reasons
why the old-timers of the Butte came to respect his shrewd
judgement and wit, the trio first among them. Because of her
admiration for Naly, Valadon insisted on his taking her son out
whenever Naly was free. Utrillo took to him, spoke freely to
him and seldom made scenes in his presence.

"To begin with there was his religion," Naly said. "It was a
strange blend. For him Christ, Joan of Arc and the Curé
of Ars were the Divinity. After the 1914–18 war he took to
venerating Colonel Ronchonneau too."

Colonel Ronchonneau was a sort of Colonel Blimp of the
1914–18 war stories. Military-minded Utrillo did not understand the jokes: he took the imaginary crazy colonel for a war
hero.

"One cannot separate Utrillo from Valadon and Utter," was
Naly's opinion. "When one asks the question, Was or wasn't
Utrillo mad?, one can only answer that his eccentricities, kinks,
fads and lack of sense of responsibility were part and parcel
of the life the trio led. It was a centrifugal life. They ran from
each other all the time, Utrillo to drink, Valadon to bury herself
in her painting, and Utter to sell paintings to court young

girls and to find himself, that is to forget the little plumber. On the Butte the three of them were called the mother, the son and the unholy ghost. Their communal life was not made easy by Utrillo's pranks; on the other hand he earned the big money, so his pranks had to be tolerated. Besides, neither Valadon nor Utter set him an example of moderation, discipline or any other virtues on which a normal existence could be based.

"Because I understood him and he respected me he couldn't play the fool with me. I told him I wouldn't tolerate it if he behaved with me like an imbecile. I never had any trouble with him, though it did give him sadistic satisfaction to act the madman before an audience."

Naly had a system with Utrillo. "We are going for a stroll," he would say when he took him out, usually in the mornings. "At twelve sharp we will have a drink." Utrillo shuffled obediently at his side, dragging his feet. Nobody ruined the soles of shoes quicker than Utrillo. When he was alone he ran; if accompanied by someone else he shuffled like a child being taken unwillingly for a walk. Naly looked at his watch. "Twenty to twelve," he would say.

"Twenty minutes left," said Utrillo.

"At twelve sharp we'll have a drink."

Utrillo kept a close check on the time. He looked at every public clock they passed. He peered into every shop that was likely to have a clock. He waited for the chimes. Naly's system was to reach a bistro at one minute to noon. Had they been a few seconds late Utrillo would have made a scene. He trusted Naly because Naly kept his word. So at twelve sharp Utrillo received his drink. Then they continued their promenade.

"He came with me like a lamb," Naly said, "because he knew I would give him a drink. A friend he was walking with had once let him down. He had promised to give him a drink at a certain hour but forgot it. When Utrillo saw that the promised hour had passed he threw himself on the ground and yelled until the police came and they were both taken to the station."

There were not many people who had Naly's shrewdness. Moreover, as Utrillo's fame increased, more and more sycophants pushed their way into his presence, and when they were about, Utrillo made even less effort than usual to control himself. They were delighted. What a perfect subject for an article or a chapter in a book on Montmartre! To the ordinary man in the Montmartre street Utrillo was, of course, sheer, raving mad—the lights and shades of the human soul completely escaped them. Anyhow, didn't all the articles, books, rumours and Utrillo's behaviour confirm it?

2

Octave Mirbeau, the begetter of the Utrillo legend, died in 1917. His collection of paintings was sold at the Durand-Ruel Gallery in February 1919. Utrillo's *La maison rose,* which Mirbeau had bought from Libaude for a hundred and fifty francs, fetched a thousand francs at the sale, a colossal figure for a contemporary painting in those days. On the Butte the rag-and-bone men and the bistro keepers congratulated themselves and called it their personal victory. Had they not started Litrillo off on the golden path with their five francs and litres of wine?

In March of the same year the collection of Eugène Descaves was put up for sale in the Hôtel Drouot. A *Notre-Dame-de-Paris* fetched 1,580 francs. At one of Libaude's sales five Utrillos were sold for a total of 6,650 francs. They had cost Libaude 200 francs before the war.

"He could have sent me a box of cigars," Utrillo commented.

Utrillo was going from strength to strength. The postwar years put him firmly in the saddle. In 1922 he exhibited a painting at the Salon d'Automne, where he had not shown since 1912, when no one had taken any notice of him. Now, however, his good friend Tabarant, under his pen name *l'Imagier,* wrote in *L'Oeuvre*: "It seems that the reputation of this sharply original painter grows all the time, especially in the last three years, in spite of silly legends and sometimes excessively hurried work . . . Utrillo is perhaps the most powerfully original painter since Van Gogh. His work is not always equally good, yet, his faults notwithstanding, his unique qualities are truly admirable."

Libaude died in the same year after an abdominal operation. He stipulated in his will that the paintings he had collected should not be sold until ten years had passed, but in 1924 his daughter agreed to the sale of a hundred Utrillos. She sold them, rumour had it, for over a million francs to M. Hodebert, successor of M. Barbazanges at the picture gallery at 100 rue du Faubourg Saint-Honoré. The pictures were in a neglected state: Libaude had not looked after them.

M. Hodebert decided to exhibit the lot. His decision caused a stir in the art world. Even Utrillo's most fervent admirers were worried. What impression would those mouldy, old paintings make? What would they look like after twelve to fifteen years of "meditation" in Libaude's attic? Moreover, they had been painted between 1910 and 1914, when Utrillo was living from hand to mouth, drunk and miserable, and fame appeared unattainable. The pride the artist is expected to take in his work had been sadly lacking in that period. He had painted because he needed drinking money. Besides, nobody had had a glimpse of those paintings after Libaude had removed them from the Avenue Trudaine. What impact would a hundred Utrillos in one mass make on the public?

The exhibition was a rousing success. The paintings were masterpieces, unaffected by poverty, drink, or madness. The colours had held, and critics and public were bowled over by the pictures of the Butte, Montmagny, Sannois and Ouessant. The exhibition proved the amazing unity of Utrillo's work. An old painter of some merit was overheard saying: "Prodigious! One looks at them, then one falls flat on one's back."

Valadon persuaded Utrillo to visit the exhibition. He examined each picture, rubbed his hands, and left without saying a word.

Prices for his paintings were soaring. In 1924 a *Blue Church* from the Georges Aubry collection fetched 19,050 francs; in 1926 a *Church of Saint-Séverin* was sold for 60,000 francs— inconceivable sums in those days when paintings were not yet bought as an insurance against inflation.

His contemporaries did not fare as well as he. Chaïm Soutine lay in La Charité Hospital in the summer of 1924. He, too, was a great painter, yet his pictures fetched practically nothing. Henri-Georges Cheval visited Soutine in the hospital and undertook to see Neter, the dealer, on Soutine's behalf. He took three of Soutine's paintings to Neter, who offered a hundred francs for them. Cheval refused to sell and took the paintings back to Soutine.

"You should have thrown them into the Seine," Soutine said in despair. "That's all they're good for."

Three months after Soutine's death in 1943, Zborowski offered Carco forty thousand francs for a Soutine still life which years before Zborowski had given Carco as a present.

Utrillo's paintings, however, were fetching enormous prices; he had not to wait until death gilded his work. Yet, success had not changed him, for one night in 1924 at the height of his success and prosperity, he was brought home by the police, covered in blood, the back of his head a huge, open wound. The police said he had attempted suicide by banging his head against the wall at the station.

Utrillo had only recently returned from another stay in the nursing home in Ivry. He was in a nervous state, spending his time playing with a toy bear and a toy railway. The night of the attempted suicide he had managed to give his nurse the slip. He was arrested in the usual fashion for the usual reason and taken to the police station in the rue Dancourt.

Almost all of Utrillo's friends discounted the suicide story. They were convinced that his head was banged accidentally against the wall while he was undergoing the ritual of *passer à tabac*. "He might have hurled himself against the wall in a fit of rage," said Utter. "Maurice hated physical pain too much to attempt suicide in such a stupid fashion," said Naly. "In any case he is too religious to want to take his own life," said Valadon. Looking at Utrillo's paintings one is almost tempted to believe the version the police gave. One is reminded of Paulo Gérard's words: "One couldn't get under his skin."

The injury was so serious that it was thought that he might not survive. It was considered kind of the local police to bring him home instead of taking him to a magistrate's court: nothing could have barred his confinement for life if the police had done so. Utrillo was semiconscious, and Valadon decided to take him to the country. With the vast sums his paintings were fetching they had bought a château in the Department of the Ain. A château suited Utter down to the ground.

The trio had become too rich to travel by train and so Valadon took her bandaged son to their Château de Saint-Bernard by car. She and Utter feared that Utrillo would never be able to paint again. Indeed, he remained in a comatose state the whole summer, but by September he gradually got back to work. First he confined himself to drawing, then oils came back into their own.

He covered door panels with pictures. They did not represent Saint-Bernard: every one was a Moulin de la Galette. Since every stroke of Utrillo's brush was worth good money, the doors had become too valuable to be used simply as doors. They were sent to Paris, where they were sold for a considerable amount.

Utrillo had become a mint. "Machine à sous" was Litrillo's new nickname. All you had to do was to put a canvas on the easel, provide him with a little red wine and you could collect plenty of ready cash in the evening. As Utrillo was a prolific painter, and painting was a necessity to him, big money poured in all the time. "The best business proposition of the century," Utter boasted. "Painting meant the same to him as beads to a nervous Chinaman."

With the vast sums Utrillo was making, the life of the trio changed completely. Utter was now considered the evil genius: the blackguard who lived on his half-witted stepson's earnings, forcing poor Maurice to work and then painting Montmartre red with the proceeds. That, of course, was not true.

Firstly, Utrillo could not be allowed to handle money. If he had it, he broke out and the danger of confinement for life always lurked in the background. He had no appreciation for luxury or the good things of life. If he were given a new suit he preferred to go on wearing the old one. In short, money would have been wasted on him. Although he was nearly forty years old, all one could do with his own money was to buy him toys, provide him with musical instruments and a nurse to guard him like a prisoner.

Secondly, Utrillo and his fortune needed a manager. Nobody was better qualified for the post than his stepfather, who knew how to efface himself. Though Utter was a good painter in his own fashion, he did not try to push his work when he was dealing in Utrillos. He had finally realized that his job in the household was not that of fellow painter, but of manager. And so, the painter in him stepped into the background when he perceived Utrillo's potentialities. In any case, he was the only member of the trio who had any sense of the value of money and whose feet were firmly planted on the ground. He was a descendant of small, conscientious Hanseatic artisans who had understood the meaning of the struggle for survival. He was on to a good thing and he did not let it slip from his grasp. If prices for Utrillos were rising all the time, he was partly responsible.

Utrillo, the breadwinner, had lost his freedom in the Place de la Bourse. But Utter and Valadon could afford theirs. They played a continuous *commedia dell' arte* act according to the rules and conception of the Butte: scandal, noise, ostentation and bragging.

Utter loved everything that was expensive, noisy and luxurious. He loved it in the ostentatious, exaggerated Montmartre sense. The sort of gesture that made him happy and proud was to order six bottles of champagne in a restaurant and then tell the waiters to drink the champagne themselves. The quondam plumber's assistant had come into his own. He dressed expensively and with little taste. He wore patent-leather shoes with white spats, striped trousers, a velvet jacket and a boater. He never went out without gloves even if he was going only from the rue Cortot to the Place du Tertre. Thinking of the Château de Saint-Bernard, he dressed as he imagined a country gentleman dressed. He wore plum-coloured plus fours and gaiters as he progressed from one Montmartre bistro to another.

The money was very much to Valadon's liking too. In her model days she had moved in rich, luxury-loving circles; the long-forgotten Mousis had given her all she asked; and now she had her son, whom she had fashioned into a painter, to satisfy her whims. Her own paintings were fetching little money. She was a painters' and critics' painter. Her work was admired almost more than her son's, yet the public which had become Utrillo's public had hardly heard of her. She liked to tell the story of an admirer of Cézanne's work who went to Aix-en-Provence, where he discovered that only five persons in a hundred had heard of Cézanne.

She took her son's commercial success in her stride. It neither surprised her nor made her envious. He was a great painter and that sufficed. She might have been jealous if he had been mediocre. Anyway, now she could give rein to her eccentricity.

One day the trio went to Revillon to buy Valadon an astrakhan coat. Utter haggled, Valadon chose and Utrillo stared at the ceiling. Eventually the most expensive coat was bought, taken home and cut up for the dogs to wear in winter. Once she was asked why the dogs had to sleep on expensive fur.

"Dogs are worth more than human beings," she answered. "Besides, I puzzle my dogs. They say, 'Just look at this strange woman who give us fur coats.'"

In spite of the new-found fortune Valadon retained her bohemian ways. She never washed up or bothered about the maidservant washing up. She could look without distaste at the accumulating dirty dishes. She had the same attitude toward laundering: a visitor saw a huge pile of Utter's and Utrillo's dirty shirts piled up on a table. She was not interested in maidservants. She seldom had more than one. Chauffeurs, however, were a different matter.

She could walk out of the rue Cortot in slippers and dressing gown like an untidy housewife, then find her way down to the Opéra, where the large Hispano-Suiza hire cars were parked, waiting for rich customers to take them sightseeing or to the Bois de Boulogne. She would choose the largest of them, say, "To Saint-Bernard," and, still in dressing gown and slippers, motor down to the château.

She tired of having to pick and choose taxis, so she took one by the year. The taxi's flag was down the whole year round, and after a few such years the taxi driver bought himself a house.

When the trio travelled it was Utter who paid the hotel bill, but Valadon insisted that he leave the tipping to her. If the room cost 500 francs she tipped 3,000. She rolled 500-franc notes into tiny balls, giving one to each member of the floor staff. Then she went down in her plumed hat, her fur coat trailing along the ground, and stopping by each page boy on her way out, dropped a little ball into his palm.

Yet not everybody was impressed by Utrillo's success. Jean-Gabriel Daragnès, the painter and engraver, who lived on the Butte, had a secondhand piano in his studio, and Utrillo came from time to time to knock out tunes on it. Daragnès bought a cheap, mass-produced wardrobe from Dufayelle's (where Utrillo had his first short-lived job). Finding himself alone with the wardrobe in the studio, Utrillo could not resist painting views of Montmartre on the panels. When Daragnès returned home he shouted: "Oh, *nom de Dieu!* what have you done to my wardrobe? Disgraceful . . . If you weren't a friend I'd make you buy another wardrobe, but as you are I won't insist. Rub off that stuff at once."

And famous Utrillo, whose canvases were feverishly sought after by dealers and collectors, humbly scratched out his four landscapes.

Utrillo was not yet known in all quarters, however. In the late twenties Ambroise Vollard, that outstanding art dealer and connoisseur, saw in the window of a picture gallery a cathedral by Utrillo, whose name was unknown to him. Here is a painter to launch, Vollard said to himself. He went in and asked the price.

"Fifty thousand francs," was the answer.

3

Utter bought the Château de Saint-Bernard in 1923. It was a crumbling old castle but it had a moat and a drawbridge. Utter and Valadon loved the moat; Utrillo remained indifferent to it. Though the château was bought with his earnings he did not fancy himself as a châtelain. He left that to Utter. But it should not be imagined that they led their lives like lords of the manor. It was merely rue Cortot transplanted to the department of the Ain. They did not want to impress the owners of other châteaux; they only wished to impress their friends on the Butte; and they were not consistent even in that.

The château lies in beautiful country near the river Saône. Utter had his studio in the annex; Valadon and Utrillo had theirs on different floors of the tower. Édouard Herriot, the French statesman and Mayor of Lyons, often came to see them. He called them "a trinity animated by the cult of art."

After crossing the moat by the drawbridge, one entered the château by a door facing the chimney piece in the enormous hall. The draught rushed in as the door opened; dust and bits of paper rose from the boards and flew up the chimney. The rain came in. It was well-nigh impossible to spend a night there. The trio really lived in the annex, where they also put up their friends. There was very little cutlery, napery and linen. The château was neither well appointed nor was life in it properly organized.

The trio had brought with them a housekeeper, Annette Jacquinot, who was not impressed by the lords and the lady of the manor. "Here in Saint-Bernard there is nothing," she complained in a letter. "No paper, no ink, and very little bread." In winter you had to break the ice in the frozen well. The château was infested with rats, field mice and owls. Jacquinot and Utter did not get on together.

Jacquinot, Utter told Naly, thought Utrillo a complete idiot and treated him as such. When the two of them were alone in Saint-Bernard, she put a dog collar round Utrillo's neck and chained him to a tree, so afraid was she that he might escape. When she unfastened him she walked him round the garden still on the chain. Now and then Utrillo was dragged along on all fours. "Utrillo accepted all that without pleasure or anger," Utter said.

A wine merchant of the locality who was well acquainted with Utrillo's drinking habits decided to exploit him. He armed himself with bow and arrow and crossed the drawbridge. He planted himself under Utrillo's window and waited till the painter opened it. Then the merchant shot an arrow into the room and Utrillo found the attached paper with the merchant's order written on it: a *Rue du Mont-Cenis* or a *Moulin de la Galette* or a *Sacré-Coeur*. In the evening the merchant returned, and Utrillo let down on a string the painting he had ordered. The merchant then tied a bottle of wine to the string. By this device the wine merchant acquired fourteen landscapes. Utter became suspicious when he found that Utrillo was not turning out enough paintings. Utter hid in the garden. His reward came in the evening when happy Utrillo lowered a new landscape from his window.

The trio had a motorcar, a Panhard-Levassor, and a chauffeur dressed in white flannels. The chauffeur often acted as warder when Utter and Valadon were away. He took Utrillo for long drives. Utrillo rode in the tonneau, exposing himself whenever they roared past a woman. The car was of the same make as the official vehicle of the Prefect of Police. Valadon tore up Utrillo's military book (*livret militaire*), saying: "There is no more need for it now that we have the same car as the Prefect," an argument difficult to follow.

Utrillo often managed to escape from the château, too. There was little danger of the authorities in Paris hearing of his short-lived escapades. When Jean Metthey, the art dealer, went to Saint-Bernard, he found Utrillo drinking in a nearby bistro. But he went like a lamb when he was discovered.

Utter brought Adolphe Basler, the art critic, to the château. "Gentle but infinitely morose," was Basler's description of Utrillo, who had immediately asked him how many stripes the art critic thought he would be entitled to if painters had ranks like soldiers.

When Utrillo was forty-five, he received his rank: he was made an officer of the Legion of Honour. Herriot had recommended him. A crowd of admirers, led by the painter Charles Senard who was Deputy Mayor of Lyons, descended on Saint-Bernard for the occasion.

"You have no decorations, have you?" Utrillo asked his mother, while they were waiting for Senard and the ribbon.

"In the name of the President of the Republic . . ." Senard began according to custom, and Utrillo stood to attention. When the ribbon was pinned to his lapel he gave a military salute. Utter said he never saw anything funnier.

"Now you are happy, Maurice," Valadon said after the ceremony. "Look, what a pretty ribbon you have."

"Do you really think that red suits me?" Utrillo asked anxiously.

Later he said he would have preferred the lilac ribbon with the academic palms, a decoration given by the Minister of Education. None the less, he was pleased with the ribbon even if red was not his favourite colour. He poked his head out of the window, shouting, "I am Maurice Utrillo, officer of the Legion of Honour. I am Maurice Utrillo, officer of the Legion of Honour . . ."

Valadon emerged from her studio and shouted up to him: "Haven't you finished yet? You make us all sick with your idiotic behaviour."

Life in the rue Cortot had also changed. The studio was invaded by all sorts of people, hoping to discover valuable paintings which dealers had overlooked. The frequent presence of strangers gave Valadon the idea of hiding a number of paintings in a wardrobe in order to keep them away from prying eyes. She showed the contents of the wardrobe to Tabarant, swearing that she would not allow even dealers to see them. Tabarant said jokingly that she would; and he was often right. To possess a *Utrillo de l'armoire* became a status symbol among collectors. However well guarded the wardrobe was, paintings managed to vanish from it. Some disappeared without trace. The wardrobe was then restocked.

In about 1926 Valadon and Utter decided to move from the rue Cortot. The studio was too small and modest for the owners of Saint-Bernard. The Avenue Junot, which rises from the rue de Caulaincourt to the Butte, had recently been constructed— it cuts across the old Maquis—and the trio chose to have a villa built there. Speculators were busily building "bijou residences" in the new avenue which the local wags called a strategic road because it enabled the police to reach the Butte more quickly and easily when fighting broke out in a bistro. They chose a small, prosperous-looking villa in a new, genteel neighbourhood. Though they never intended to give up their noisy, turgid existence, the villa was added proof of the trio's longing for bourgeois respectability.

The locked wardrobe gave Utter a capital idea. He signed a contract with the Bernheim-Jeune Gallery for Utrillo's work, and the capital idea was for Bernheim-Jeune to finance the construction of the new home. The partners wanted to see the contents of the wardrobe. They were entitled to do so since the contract stipulated that all sales should go through them; and Utrillos were, after all, painted to be sold. Utter said to Bernheim-Jeune: "You will have the contents of the wardrobe if you build us a new studio in the Avenue Junot. Though we intend to keep it, the one in the rue Cortot is too small for us." M. Bernheim-Jeune went with Utter to choose the ground; he also found them an architect. The villa was built without the dealer setting eyes on the paintings in the wardrobe. The wardrobe was opened only after the villa was ready for the trio to move in. Bernheim-Jeune did not regret the deal.

Downstairs the villa contained passage, kitchen, dining room and a big studio for Utter; upstairs were two small cell-like rooms, one Utrillo's bedroom with an iron bedstead, the other his studio. A large bedroom was on the other side of the landing and in the garden, only six feet from the Moulin de la Galette, was Valadon's studio. Utrillo's rooms had bars on the windows.

Utrillo was carefully guarded; none the less he succeeded in breaking out even from the villa. He knew they would be looking for him everywhere on the Butte and in Low Montmartre, so he took the *métro*, got out at a distant station, surfaced, then ran into the first bistro, where he had a drink. He dived back into the *métro* and travelled to another distant station, where the same tactics were repeated. He often changed lines to put his pursuers off the scent. When he felt drunk enough he staggered home to his warders. He did not dare any longer to stay out the whole night.

One could do little with him: he had all the toys and musical instruments he wanted. His behaviour did not improve. He exposed himself even in front of his mother's female visitors, shouting, "I paint with this." He did the same at the window when he saw a woman passing the villa. He had acquired an air pistol with which he threatened female passers-by. If they ran he shook with happy laughter.

A postwoman of Montmartre used to deliver parcels to the villa now and then. She pushed a small, three-wheeled post-office barrow. She wore laced boots reaching up to her knees, a dark-blue plaited skirt, a short jacket and a red, white and blue pompom on her peaked cap. When Utrillo heard the barrow approaching he became enormously excited and rushed to the window shouting, "Filthy whore!"

One morning he managed to get out into the avenue. He rushed after her and she ran away pushing her barrow, laughing and shrieking, "Litrillo, Litrillo. He's mad, he's mad."

"It was perhaps the only idyll of his life," said Utter, who maintained that Utrillo was in love with the postwoman and calling her a filthy whore was his way of expressing his ardent love. The schoolboy again.

The guests who were allowed into Utrillo's studio found him either embarked on a canvas, painting from a picture postcard, calculating the dimensions with a compass or playing with his electric train. Though he was severely rationed one could not get anything out of him without first promising him a drink. If Valadon wanted him to behave decently in front of a visitor she had to offer him a little wine.

In the same year when the trio moved into their new abode in the Avenue Junot, Diaghilev produced Balanchine's ballet *Barabeau* at the Théâtre Sarah Bernhardt. Scenery and costumes were designed by Utrillo. The scenery was the church of Saint-

Bernard, the costumes came straight off the backs of the figures in any Utrillo painting.

By then Utrillo, at forty-three, had ceased to be inventive. To many creative artists lack of inventiveness comes even earlier. With Utrillo it was only the end of the adventure but not of the talent. All he does, said his ill-wishers, is to copy his own work. None the less, Utrillo copied Utrillo remarkably well.

Utrillo's Marriage and Valadon's Death

1

M. AND MME. PAUWELS visited Berthe Weill's gallery shortly after the 1919 armistice and bought several paintings by Utrillo and Valadon. "Here are the new collectors," wrote Weill. "They buy good paintings but snobbism enters into it too much. They are too impatient, waiting for the value of their pictures to rise."

Robert Édouard Pauwels was a well-mannered, kindly man. He was thought to be rich; he himself believed that he was, but his fortune was not as solid as he and his wife gave one to think. His health was not good. His wife, Françoise Alexandrine Jeanne Lucie Veau, was born on March 18, 1878. Her father was a small vine grower, her mother a dressmaker whose shop faced the cathedral of Angoulême. Lucie was educated in a modest convent school. She believed that she was destined for the stage. As a young girl, so she said, she had played Dorine in

Tartuffe before Coquelin, the legendary French actor, in Bordeaux. Her sturdily provincial parents were against her embarking on an actress' career. But there appeared on the scene Joseph Bernaud, a young sculptor from Paris, who assisted in the cleaning of the cathedral walls. As the Veau family lived opposite the cathedral he met Lucie, who was then twenty-three years of age. She left with him for Paris, where they were married on September 28, 1901.

Lucie adopted the stage name of Lucie Valore. When the Great War broke out she found herself with a theatrical troupe in Belgium, where she met M. Pauwels. He married her in 1915. She said she was on the Brussels stage at the time of her marriage, but it is difficult to believe that the Germans would have permitted an enemy touring company to perform in German-occupied territory. When the war ended Pauwels and Valore established themselves in the Avenue Mozart in Paris. He gambled heavily on the Bourse, owned race horses and they entertained handsomely. They told Berthe Weill that they adored artists. Once a month they gave a lavish tea and lemonade party, at which the adored artists sang or recited poetry.

Weill was invited to one of the parties. She had just come from an excellent luncheon. The contrast startled her. Whereas at the luncheon all had been wit and fun, at the Pauwels' everything was forced and artificial. The guests icily eyed each other, self-conscious and ashamed of being there in spite of all the music and poetry.

"Life is absent in this house," Weill observed.

Valore seemed an unlikely candidate to become Utrillo's only wife. She was a bulky woman with hard, uncharitable blue eyes. She brimmed over with energy, but her true strength lay in her conviction that she was cleverer than the many enemies she made. Consequently she always succeeded in turning the enemy line. There is nothing like conviction. She attacked at points from which no one in his right mind would have expected an onslaught. She was not liked yet she got her way. If she wanted something she went for it unflinchingly. She was most amiable if she needed you.

She met the trio as far back as 1919. Theirs was not an accidental meeting: she and her husband went to Montmartre with the definite aim of meeting Utrillo and Valadon. In the rue Cortot she and her husband planted themselves in front of Number 12, waiting for mother or son to appear.

Valadon was the first to appear. In her book *Maurice Utrillo, mon mari,* published after Utrillo's death, Valore describes the encounter. Valadon was carrying a sketchbook almost as large as herself. Valore's intuition told her it must be Valadon. "Mme. Suzanne Valadon, I presume?" Valore asked.

"Exactly, madame," answered Valadon. "To whom have I the pleasure of speaking?"

"Oh, madame, my name means nothing to you. I am Mme. Robert Pauwels; this is my husband."

"Mme. Pauwels!" exclaimed Valadon. "Your name means a lot to me. It is known in the studio of every painter. M. Pauwels is a renowned collector, and you, madame, are so beautiful and elegant."

Thus Valore's book. When it came out Valadon's old friends had a good laugh. She was the last person to praise another woman for her beauty, and, as for elegance, she was no more interested in other women's dresses than in her own. Valadon asked the Pauwels in, and Valore's heart beat faster as she mounted the twisting, dangerous stairs in anticipation of meeting Maurice Utrillo. He was at home. Valadon introduced the Pauwels and Utrillo thanked them for the interest they took in his work.

After that the Pauwels frequently entertained the trio in the Avenue Mozart. Utrillo would stand in the drawing room shifting from one foot to the other, taking no part in the conversation. "Say something," his mother would urge him.

"*Oui, oui,*" answered Utrillo, and continued to say nothing. But Valore came to his rescue. Taking him by the arm, she led him to the fruit cup on the dining-room table. "I'd have preferred a glass of red wine in the kitchen," Utrillo said afterward.

Utrillo was attracted by colossal Mme. Pauwels. One may not like her, one may deplore the way she treated Valadon after her marriage to Utrillo, none the less it is undeniable that she impressed the misogynist. She was the great lady from the unknown, frightening, grand world. He looked up at her as a street urchin looks at the illuminated Christmas tree in a big store. The Pauwelses led a well-regulated life; the tablecloth was not torn and the napkins were clean, unheard-of luxuries for one coming from the rue Cortot. Not that Utrillo or Valadon cared a rap about such refinements, but they found them impressive in someone else's house. They still maintained the dual standard: they were bohemians that appreciated respectability, but they would shriek in rage if it were forced on them. The Pauwelses threw their weight about. Valore was always overdressed, and her overbearing ways were bound to impress the man from whom most women fled. For Utrillo she was elegance and worldliness personified. She was also the fat woman with big buttocks straight out of his paintings.

In February 1933 Pauwels died of uremia, leaving his affairs in a mess. His widow, now fifty-five, found herself with clamouring creditors and practically no money.

Utter helped her to disentangle her late husband's affairs. Debts were paid, and all that was left was her house, La Doulce France, near Angoulême. Because Utter had been kind to Valore the story went round that he was in love with her. The story was embellished: Utter wanted to divorce Valadon in order to marry Valore. The story was amplified: Utter wanted to marry Valore so that Utrillo's earnings would keep them both after Valadon's death. Not one word was true. Utter was in love, though not with Pauwels' widow, nor his own wife.

It had been easy for a woman with Valadon's panache to sweep aside all obstacles when she married a man 21 years her junior.

She was then 49 years old. Now, however, she was way over 60 and had begun to show her age, though her spirit remained young and indomitable. It was the aging shell, so to speak, that was fiercely jealous of the comparatively young, philandering husband. And at 68 she was still as possessive as she had been at 10.

Noisy scenes were more and more frequent, both in private and public. One day Utter said to her in desperation, "When you etch you have only to spit on the copper. Your spittle will eat into it."

To be able to appreciate Valadon's reactions to the energetic widow, two points should be borne in mind. Firstly, Valadon's health was failing; and secondly, she still loved Utter with the possessiveness she had always shown. But Utter was no longer living with her and was in love with another woman. He was back in the rue Cortot in their old studio.

Utter's new love had once been the trio's secretary. She had a respectable bourgeois background. Before she took her job in the Avenue Junot, she had separated from her husband, an important civil servant. She was not good looking, but had distinguished features. In England she would probably have been a hunting woman given to country and county pursuits. As she was French she ended up as an art dealer. She was of the same world as the trio: her manners were excellent; she was invariably urbane. She was called Yvette. She had an aquiline nose and dressed severely. Utter thought her the acme of good breeding. In deference to her, his ties became more sober, his spats even whiter and he took to wearing a monocle. Valadon despised him for his newfangled snobbery. "Poor little plumber!" she said.

However, Utter did not leave Valadon entirely. Nobody could. He went almost every day to the Avenue Junot when he was in Paris, and when he could not go himself he sent friends like Jean Dufy, the painter, or Naly to look after her. Valadon did not forgive him, yet that did not stop her from discussing her problems with him. The visits invariably ended with quarrelling and shouting. She nagged him as though they were still together.

It soon became apparent that Valore was after Utrillo, the best business proposition of the century, as Utter had said. Valore had the habit of consulting fortunetellers. In 1935 she went to see an eminent member of that popular calling, who declared: "The cards tell me that you will marry a great man. Your past life is nothing compared to the one you will lead beside the choice of your heart . . . A husband who will dearly love you, and you will look after him as one looks after a child." To be on the safe side Valore visited a second prophetess who said: "Madame, you will marry a man of great worth, known, loved and admired by the entire world, though he does not belong to it. He loves you in silence. Through him you will be in the public eye and even become famous yourself."

Valore had no idea to whom the fortunetellers referred; none the less she visited the Avenue Junot more assiduously than before.

Valadon suspected nothing; that is, she had no time to suspect anything because she was too upset and enraged by Utter's behaviour. He put on airs that drove Valadon to fury. He viewed the villa with disdain. He more or less told Valadon that her unorganized existence and bohemian outlook were not up to his standards. He found the noise she made rather vulgar. She gave him tit for tat, calling him a plumber's mate, an upstart and a ridiculous figure. He returned the next day to say more and to receive more; and so it went.

"It was really like seeing an ungrateful son rowing with his mother," Jean Dufy said.

Utter took Yvette to Saint-Bernard and Valadon followed them. Utter swore that while he and Yvette were asleep, Valadon had their bedroom walled up, and thus kept them prisoners for several days. If they wanted food they let down a basket into which Valadon put boiled cabbage. "That was all we had to eat for nearly a week," Utter said.

"Didn't you hear the masons at work?" he was asked.

"We were too much in love," replied Utter.

Valore quietly watched as the life-edifice of the trio crumbled to bits. Early in 1935 Valadon was in the American Hospital in Neuilly, suffering from diabetes and uremia. Valore visited her in the hospital. They spoke of Utrillo. The sick mother was worried, for what would become of her son if she died? Utter would no longer look after him, and Maurice could not be left alone, for the authorities would step in at once and confine him in an asylum for life. Moreover, he had neither the strength nor the experience to look after himself. Even his outbursts were not as formidable as in the past. In the weak state she was in, Valadon thought that Valore and Utrillo's marriage would be the best way out for him. Valore was delighted. She told everybody that it was Valadon's wish that she should marry Utrillo.

After leaving the hospital Valadon denied that she had ever said such a thing. She was comparatively strong again, and did not care to remember how morally weak she had been.

Jean Metthey was Utrillo's and Valadon's art dealer at the time. He was a delightful man and a shrewd observer, to whom Utrillo was deeply attached.

"The situation was this," Metthey said when recalling those stormy days. "Everything had fallen to pieces. Valadon alone remained. It was probably her greatest period in oils. The nearer death came, the better she painted. Just think of her flower paintings. She went on developing all the time. With Maurice it was the opposite. He had stopped developing long ago. At his best he made admirable copies of his own work. As a person he had reached the stage where one could push him about as one wanted. The interesting thing is that he needed painting more than his mother, because painting was the only outlet left to him.

"Into the shattered life caused by Utter's departure entered Valore. Maurice hated change but now there seemed no alternative. Valadon couldn't make up her mind either. One minute she thought that Valore was the only solution for her son, the next she said the most horrible things of her. All in front of Maurice. I know, since I walked him out every Sunday. When Valore took him away, that is, when she took him to Angouléme, my standing joke was that I had arranged the marriage because I was tired of walking him out on Sundays. If she had come while Utter was still in the house she wouldn't have stood a chance."

One afternoon Naly went to the Avenue Junot and found Valadon in her studio. Valore was upstairs with Utrillo. On a shelf in the studio stood a small bottle of wine Valadon had promised Utrillo, but when she saw him approaching with Valore she hid the wine and put a bottle of Vittel water in its place.

"You mustn't do that," Naly said. "With Maurice you have to keep your word. This is like breaking a contract."

"So you're going to marry this creature," were Valadon's first words as they entered the studio. "Look at her with her hanging breasts . . . and now you're going to marry her."

Utrillo stopped before the bottle of Vittel water. "Have I gone mad?" he asked.

"You are not mad, I am mad," exploded Valadon. "Only a madwoman could have painted that picture." She pointed to the fine canvas showing herself, her mother, Utter and Utrillo. "The family! There is no family left. I, your mother, am mad; you are just an idiot. One needs spirit and intelligence to be mad. You aren't intelligent. If you were, you wouldn't want to marry this woman. You are not entitled to call yourself mad."

Valore swallowed much in a good cause. But the next day, Valadon was all for the marriage again. Then she was furious because Valore dared to call her son *"mon chéri, mon grand maître."* Utrillo addressed Valore as *"ma grande fiancée."*

Valadon told Valore that her son was impotent. Valore's reply was that the late M. Pauwels had been a sick man for a considerable time, so she was accustomed to an abstemious life.

Naly and Jean Dufy warned Valadon that Valore would

carry off Utrillo. "Look out," said Naly. "If she gets him as far as Angoulême she will marry him and that will be the end of the trio."

"There is nothing left of the trio," said Valadon. "André saw to that."

"You'll starve if she grabs Maurice," Naly said. He had sold a painting for her for the paltry sum of two hundred and fifty francs only a few days before. It had been hard work to get even as much as that.

"But up there they will starve too," said Valadon, meaning Utter and Yvette in the rue Cortot.

"Up there" Utter understood all the implications. No one appreciated more than he that his easy life would be at an end if Valore triumphed. Yet he did little about it. He was too much in love with Yvette. Everything was working in Valore's favour.

"It lies between marrying Utrillo and starting a picture gallery," Valore confided in Metthey.

Marrying Utrillo turned out to be the easier proposition. In April 1935 Valore decided to strike. She went to the Avenue Junot accompanied by her nephew. To their surprise it was Utter who opened the door. He wanted to bar their way. Utrillo, he announced, would be taken to Lyons to stay with friends: marriage could be discussed at a later date. Valore was furious. She accused Utter and Valadon of treating her disgracefully. She was sick of the whole comedy; no one had the right to behave as badly as they.

While she spoke she propelled her imposing bulk into the house. She caught sight of Utrillo on the landing. "They want to take me away from you," he vociferated, "but be assured that I will marry you. I love you, I love you, Lucie."

"Help! Help!" Valadon shrieked from an upstairs window. "Murder! Murder!"

Utter had pushed Valore and her nephew out of the house.

"When Valore and her nephew had gone," Metthey said, "Valadon turned on Utter, blaming him for everything. Infuriated, he left the house. Then in my presence Valadon told her son that the best thing for him to do was to marry the fat woman straight out of his painting. In any case one couldn't keep the trio together any longer. I thought, let Valore take him and then there will be a little peace and quiet at last. So I went down to the *brasserie* to calm Valore."

Metthey found Valore and her nephew in the *brasserie* at the bottom of the avenue. Valore, still trembling all over, ordered a cordial. When Metthey appeared, he told her not to take it too seriously; surely she knew them well enough by now, and if she came back in a couple of days' time she would see that everything had blown over.

Before returning to the Avenue Junot Valore went in search of Utter. It was not difficult to search for anyone on the Butte. She ran him down in La Bonne Franquette, a restaurant in the rue des Saules. Utter and Valore had a violent row, Utter accusing her of wanting to snatch Utrillo because of the money, Valore riposting that Utter had lived long enough on Utrillo's earnings. Utter held out longer, in that Valore was the first to leave. Then he turned to those present in the restaurant and made the remark which became famous and was quoted for years on the Butte: "The firm of Utrillo has changed hands."

He sold one of the last Utrillos he had and arranged to take Yvette on a Mediterranean cruise. The road was clear—cleared by Utter.

When he spoke of the marriage he frankly admitted that he had not played his cards well. "But it was also a relief," he added, "to let someone else worry about him, guard him and keep him quiet. I had had it for twenty-five years."

"What one must bear in mind when speaking of Utrillo and Valore," Jean Dufy observed, "is that Utrillo thought his mother didn't care for him any more. That was the conclusion the simpleton drew from her ambiguous attitude. If she still loved him, he reasoned, she would not let anyone come between them and would send Valore packing."

The next day Valore went to the Avenue Junot. Valadon received her with open arms, insisting on her staying for luncheon. Valadon had already heard that Utter and his mistress were leaving on a cruise, and she told Valore that she could take Utrillo away. The whole idea of Lyons, she added, had emanated from Utter, who wanted poor Maurice to go on painting for his friends without being paid for it. "Just look, he's going on a cruise now," Valadon said, turning to her son. "Your place is beside your fiancée." She beamed at Valore. "I know that he will be happy with you." They had kidneys for lunch, Utrillo's favourite dish.

Utrillo embraced his mother and left with Valore. A car was waiting for them at the foot of the avenue. Valore left nothing to chance. On April 14, Palm Sunday, Utrillo painted the house of St. Joan of Arc in Domrémy from a postcard and wrote beneath, "Voices councilled Joan of Arc. The same voices led me to Lucie Valore." They were married at the Mairie of the 16th *arrondissement* on April 18, then they departed for Angoulême. "Long live liberty," were, according to Valore, Utrillo's last words when he left his mother. And so he had finally left the woman he had lived with for over fifty years, the woman who had made a painter of him. There was, however, no liberty for him, neither long- nor short-lived. He had simply moved from one bondage to another.

Paulo Gérard said Utrillo was like a folding chair. Valore had folded it up and carried it to La Doulce France.

The evening after their departure Naly looked in on Valadon. "Where is Maurice?" he asked.

"Maurice has gone off with her. I told him to."

"You are clever. What will you do now? Starve?"

"They'll starve too up there," Valadon said.

A few days later she repented. Her son had no right to leave her. It was she who had protected him and saw to it that he fulfilled his vocation as a painter in the same fashion as she had done. But then came the other woman who took him away. "I never believed that he could leave me," she said to Michelle Deroyer, the writer. "We were too miserable for that."

There Valadon certainly scored a point. What was Utrillo leaving behind? Two cell-like rooms, constant supervision, quarrels, and his toys. Valore would give him new ones. But, in addition, he would lose the Butte, for Valore would never let him settle there again. Still that mattered little: he carried Montmartre with him wherever he went, as his paintings showed.

"I've discovered why Maurice married her," Valadon went on to Michelle Deroyer. "Because she looks like the big-arsed women in his paintings. And to think that she is my daughter-in-law . . . my daughter-in-law! I feel like saying my mother-in-law."

The religious ceremony took place in the church of Saint-Ausonne in Angoulême. Utrillo and Valore were married by Monsignor Palmer and their union blessed by Monsignor Megnin, the Bishop of Angoulême. The Prefect of Charente was Utrillo's witness. Valore's was Pajot, the sculptor.

"There were archbishops at my son's wedding," said Valadon. "There wasn't all that fuss when he was born."

Surely, neither Utrillo nor Valore could be held responsible for that.

2

Utrillo was no longer in Montmartre when I went to live on the Butte in 1936. Valore still kept him at La Doulce France. They were soon to return north, but not to the streets and trees, houses and cobbles which called him so clearly to mind. She bought a decent bourgeois house, which had belonged to Bourdelle the sculptor, at Le Vésinet in the department of Seine et Oise, eighteen kilometers from Paris. It was like changing from a three-masted schooner to a paddle steamer plying between holiday resorts.

Yet in spirit Utrillo remained on the Butte, more so than the other members of his generation who had also left. Picasso, Raoul Dufy, Max Jacob, Van Dongen had all gone. Carco came up from time to time. The new generation of painters and writers carried on the tradition deriving from the great days of the Lapin Agile. One drank as hard as those who went before. However, drinking was now concentrated in the Place du Tertre, which was not yet a mart for tourists. Utter was the crowned head, Naly his alter ego. I was soon steeped in Utrillo lore. Nobody seemed to speak of anybody else.

"Valadon exists," I remember Daragnès saying, "but there is no Utrillo. We invented him. There is no Utrillo, only a world of Utrillo." He turned to Carco. "It was you, Dorgelès, Warnod and the others who created him. Utrillo never said anything memorable in his life."

"Still there is the legend," Carco said.

I can hardly remember a meal where Utrillo, Valadon and Valore were not discussed; Utrillo the shadow, the other two very much in the light. Utter never spoke ill of Utrillo. Before Valore's arrival on the scene, the trio's adventures, extravagances and eccentricities were discussed good-humouredly. But now, sides were taken. There was a Valadon Party, an Utter Party and a Valore Party which, naturally, was the most active of the three. The partisans of the lady who held the purse strings spread the lie that Valadon had been a bad mother. They went as far as to say Valadon drank, which was completely untrue. Naly and Jean Dufy had often been present when she begged Utter not to drink in front of Utrillo—afraid he'd set a bad example. The Valore Party had its knife in Utter. The Valadon Party and the Utter Party fought against the insinuations emanating from Le Vésinet. All those I associated with belonged either to the Valadon or the Utter Party or occasionally to both.

Life on the Butte was easy. There was always one of us who had enough for wine or a meal. If everybody was broke then it was chalked up. I moved into the only modern house in the

Place du Tertre, Number 13, but I hardly ever had a meal in
my flat. I would come out with the intention of doing some
shopping, and lo! there they all were outside La Mère Catherine
or the Cadet de Gascogne so, of course, I joined them, and that
was the end of all sober intentions. Yet I managed to write my
first novel, *Angry Man's Tale*, on the Butte.

I had already had glimpses of Valadon in different restaurants
of the Butte. When you are young you are not overwhelmed
by greatness. All I saw was a small, vivacious, aging woman who
wore spectacles, thick stockings and always the same raincoat,
and seemed to talk most of the time. Like the general public I
was moved by Utrillo's painting: not yet by hers. That was to
come only after the war when I went to the Musée National de
l'Art Moderne and saw the Hommage à Suzanne Valadon exhibition. There I bitterly regretted that I had not taken her in
more on the only occasion we dined together, which was about
six months before her death.

We were six at a table in the Moulin Joyeux. I sat between
Jean Dufy and Jean Metthey.

"I hear," Valadon said, addressing me, "that you are a writer."

"I've had my first novel accepted," I said proudly.

"Think of all the years you will have to keep it up," Valadon
said. "One should start in old age. Then one needn't worry."

I was not impressed.

Later I heard her say, "I can't go to Saint-Bernard any more.
He has poisoned the well."

"Who?" I asked Jean Dufy.

"André, of course," laughed Jean Dufy.

That is all I remember.

Luckily it was different in the case of Utrillo. At that time
Creixams had a studio in the rue Gabrielle and there I met
Utrillo, who was then living in Le Vésinet with Valore.

Creixams was fundamentally a good painter, but he made
enough money for eating, dressing and loving, according to his
excellent taste, by painting Spanish gypsy women, which added

little to his art. I admired his engravings. One afternoon I came to the studio and Creixams said: "Maurice Utrillo is coming here. Don't make any sudden movement or gesture. He is petrified by a sudden movement. It reminds him of the times he was arrested."

"What about you?" I asked. Creixams made gestures that would have reminded Don Quixote of the windmills and caused him to charge forthwith.

"He is not afraid of me. He fears only strangers. Anyway, I never gesture."

Valore, I gathered, was to leave Utrillo in the studio while she attended to some important business connected with an exhibition. She had asked Creixams on the telephone to give Utrillo watered wine only. They arrived, I was introduced, Valore went and Utrillo remained standing in the doorway, rubbing his hands. He shook hands with me, taking mine in both of his, though he did not press hard nor look at me.

"Come, sit down, Maurice," said Creixams, putting out his right hand to take him by the arm. Utrillo recoiled. Creixams stepped forward, Utrillo started backing toward the landing, so Creixams backed away to give him confidence. Utrillo came forward, Creixams grabbed his arm, Utrillo jumped. Creixams gave him his huge, warm smile and said coaxingly, "I have wine for you, Maurice. Good, ordinary *pinard*." I was a lonely figure in the window. Creixams called to me to sit down with them. We sat at the small table with Spanish gypsy women staring at us from every canvas. We drank watered wine, but as Creixams was a *caballero* the wine was not that watered. Now and then Creixams hit Utrillo on the shoulder in his exuberant manner. Utrillo winced.

I had, of course, expected Utrillo to look and behave as he did. I do not think there existed anybody on the Butte who did not know everything that was to be known about him. After all, his life had been rather in the public eye in Montmartre before he was taken to Le Vésinet. Even so I was astonished. He reminded me of an incredibly seedy actor who hadn't seen work for a long time, yet what struck me most was the "essence" of him—as though he were made of indiarubber, no bones, only rubber. He wore an expensive suit, yet did not appear to be well dressed. The red ribbon of the Legion of Honour was sewn to his lapel. He was shaved, which I understood was unusual. His pale blue eyes were on the door. He closed them when he drank, and he drank little. His Adam's apple was very much in evidence. You felt in a vacuum with him.

And then suddenly he became interested in me. "How tall are you?" he asked. I said I was one meter eighty-nine. "I am one meter seventy-four," Utrillo said. He returned to the subject a little later. "One meter and eighty-nine centimeters is very tall."

The next time I saw him he asked me again how tall I was. One day I was lunching at La Bonne Franquette. Utrillo sat with Valore and Naly at the next table. They called me over and Utrillo asked me how tall I was, then volunteered the information that he was one meter seventy-four. The very last time I saw him, which was in the early fifties, he was in his car in the Place du Tertre; I was in a bar, and Valore came in and called me out. Utrillo sat in deep gloom in the tonneau, looking not as much ravaged as savaged by the years. "You must be very tall," he said. They drove away before he could concentrate on asking for my exact height.

"He is a writer," said Creixams at that first meeting, poking me in the rib.

"I am really a writer myself," Utrillo said.

"You are a painter and a great one," laughed Creixams, poking him in the rib. Utrillo jumped.

Their conversation was roughly on these lines:

"Do you remember so and so?" Creixams asked.

"I remember everybody," Utrillo said.

A little later Creixams said: "I saw your old friend so and so the other day."

"Who? I don't think I know him. I don't remember him."

Here, I thought, was a man who was born a wreck, lived like a wreck, yet achieved fulfillment in his art, the wreck triumphant, the embodiment of victory over all rules and regulations—no cautionary tale for children.

"So you are a writer?" Utrillo said, turning back to me. I said I was. "I am really a writer myself," he went on, "but I haven't time to write or read. Who was the writer who never read? There was one, I know."

We could not help him, so he became a little agitated and Creixams gave me a warning look. "There was one," Utrillo insisted. "He only wrote but never read."

"I saw Carco the other day," Creixams quickly said. "We dined together."

"That man had his reasons for not reading," said Utrillo.

"Have you seen Carco of late?" Creixams asked.

"It is strange for a man only to write and not to read," said Utrillo.

Then he lost all interest in the man who only wrote but never read, and asked Creixams after the health of a mutual acquaintance. Creixams said he was well, but Utrillo had ceased listening. Then Valore came to fetch him with loud endearing words and he was more than ready to go.

"I was afraid he might make a scene," said Creixams, wiping his forehead.

"Is he always like this?" I could not help asking.

"I have known him for donkey's years," said Creixams, "and when he is not drunk he is always like this. When he is drunk then God help you. Don't forget he is now only the shadow of his old self. Mind you, he has always been more or less a shadow."

Daragnès was right, I thought. Utrillo the man existed only in the conversations and anecdotes about him. I had to admit that all who held that Utrillo had never said anything memorable were also right. However, that did not dampen my admiration for the painter. I was deeply moved to have met that great claustrophobic painter, who was a supreme master of space, and whose paintings had taught me how to look at houses and streets. You have only to look down the rue du Mont-Cenis or up the rue Tholozé to appreciate the gift of perspective Utrillo gives away with each canvas. "What a beautiful thing perspective is," Uccello exclaimed five hundred years ago, waking up his wife in the middle of the night. Utrillo had made perspective a beautiful thing for me.

"They say," said Jean Dufy when I told him of my meeting with Utrillo, "that he and his mother and André are accursed painters, accursed in the sense that Lautrec was accursed as a painter and Nerval as a poet. Maurice isn't an accursed painter. He wanted two things from life: drink and painting. He got them both."

"What goes on in his mind?" an American girl asked me that night. She was an admirer of Utrillo's work. "Does he think?"

"His mind," I replied, "consists of churches, houses and streets. Isn't that enough?"

3

With her son gone, life for Valadon was simpler if lonelier. The heavy responsibility to the authorities weighed no longer on her shoulders. When the Valore Party called her a bad mother, they willfully forgot how difficult it had been to act as Utrillo's constant warder. Utrillo had always had a surprise up his sleeve.

Even after his departure she still had nightmares about the old days in the rue Cortot, when she had to fetch her Maurice home, covered in mud, bleeding and gesticulating, while the old women of the neighbourhood watched. "I was pale, furious, desperate, and wished my son were small again," she said. Although he had left behind an awful memory, she missed him and even the misery he caused her.

The money situation did not worry her. Valadon was above

that. Neither her mind nor her temperament accepted compromise with the fleshpots. There had been lots of money: now there was none. She was born poor, she said, and would die in the same state as she was born. When the gas company threatened to cut her off because she had not paid the bill, she made an unforgettable remark which almost sums her up: "They surely wouldn't do that to a person who has been their customer for fifty years."

After Utrillo's departure Valadon deserted her studio in the garden and painted in Utrillo's cell. "It is here," she said to a visitor, "that Maurice, drawing from memory or after cheap postcards, created the enchanting poems that are his canvases."

In her last years she painted mostly flowers. Models, she explained, were too expensive, unpunctual and boring to have around. Of her own painting she observed to Michelle Deroyer: "I don't understand the experts, neither their explanations nor their comparisons. When they speak of technique, balance and values they simply make me dizzy. Only two things exist for me and all others who paint: good pictures and bad pictures, that's all."

She once said to a painter who set up his easel at the corner of the rue des Saules, a forerunner of the present-day mass-producers of Montmartre landscapes, "A good painter can paint bad pictures, but a bad painter can't paint good ones."

She was still stunned by the events, partly engendered by herself, that led up to her son's marriage. "Whatever he did," she said, "wherever he went to get drunk, his one guiding thought was to return to his mother. But now he is definitely lost. The umbilical cord is torn. How can you expect me not to think of it for the rest of my life?"

Because she no longer had Utrillo and because she needed someone, all her love was now transferred to Gazi le Tartar. "He is a Crimean prince," she told everyone.

Gazi was a short, unkempt man with Tartar features, a painter of snowy landscapes. One day we stood side by side in the Place du Tertre with the sun beating down bright and harsh, the square practically sparkling from the light on the coloured umbrellas above the restaurant tables. "I imagine you see this all covered in snow," I said. "Snow is pure," Gazi said gravely.

He always wore the same soft hat covered with grease spots, and carried a cane which he lifted to the brim of the hat in salutation. If I think of him I see his profile cut in two, as it were, by the cane. I seldom saw him without the same old shopping bag.

Gazi called Valadon *"Mémère."* She loved him, he declared, for reasons that already existed before his birth. It was God's will that they should meet. Their strange relationship made many people snigger. *Mémère,* the old woman, and her adopted son were the butt of the local wags. Yet because of his blatant sincerity, I for one cannot disbelieve Gazi when he spoke of their souls being joined together, even though he was a stranger in her family.

He was in and out of the villa in his old coat almost every day. So was Utter, who continued watching over Valadon in spite of the quarrels, rows and abuse each visit provoked. She could not get over the fact that he no longer loved her with the passion of twenty-five years ago. In Yvette she saw a witch, for only a witch could have come between her, a woman of over seventy, and her husband.

Utter was worried about her and asked Naly to look in on her after dinner. She had been seriously ill, and what would happen if she had another bout when she was all alone in the house? After a while he persuaded Naly to sleep there. Naly was given Utrillo's rickety bed. The bedstead was being devoured by woodworm.

Naly made up the fire, looked after the central heating, also did a bit of cleaning as Valadon had no servant, not even a charwoman. Her nerves were bad; she complained all the time, reiterating that she had nothing to fight for since she had lost her son. Naly believed she accepted his nightly presence because she loved to listen to stories, especially to stories of adventure. Naly had just came back from Abyssinia. She sat up late into the night insisting on his telling her tales of his journey.

"Raconte-moi, raconte-moi," she said when he stopped.

But it was she who told most of the stories. Her father, she averred, was a famous bandit in Auvergne who was guillotined in 1840. Naly pointed out that she was born in the 1860s but she stuck to her tale.

There was trouble with the coal. She had no money, and it fell to Jean Metthey, who was still Utrillo's dealer, to supply her with coal. She was never satisfied with what the coalman delivered. If it was English coal she said she hated it because English coal was bad coal. She wanted Polish coal instead. So the coalman brought Polish coal. Then Valadon complained that she hated Polish coal, for it was bad coal. English coal was the only good coal.

Naly and Valadon used to sit in the room that had been Utter's studio. The villa was full of cats that had scratched the leather off armchairs and sofa. Valadon was devoted to the cats and knew how to produce their feline essence in the drawings she made of them. One of the kittens was named Negus in honour of Naly's Abyssinian journey. The room, like the rest of the villa, was covered in dust; bits of paper were all over the floor, and in a corner of the studio stood a broken pail. Naly could not persuade Valadon to give it to the dustman. "That pail has to stay," she said, though it served no purpose.

Valadon considered soap disgusting as it left dark marks on basins. Soap, she declared, should be used as little as possible. Instead, she used lavender water with which she rubbed her forehead, neck and hands every hour or so. She refused to have the kitchen floor swept; Naly was allowed to use only an antiseptic of her choice. Dust, she decreed, should remain unruffled, as dust contained cancer germs. Half of mankind suffered from cancer because people were foolish and ignorant enough to interfere with dust.

The tap above the sink had been deliberately broken. Naly asked Valadon who had done such a stupid thing and for what reason.

"Utter did that," Valadon explained. "The swine came here in the middle of the night while I was sleeping, smashed all the taps, then turned on the water because he wanted to drown me in my sleep."

Of course, she had smashed the tap herself.

The central heating worked irregularly and Naly looked after it when he arrived. One night, when he had gone upstairs to Utrillo's cell and was lying in bed reading, he heard the water boiling in the radiator. He found it strange, for he had not put more coal than usual into the boiler. Besides it had a damper which Naly knew he left opened. He rushed downstairs: the boiler had been stoked up after he went upstairs. It was full of coal and the damper was closed. He quickly shovelled out half the burning coal. Then he went into the dining room where Valadon was sitting with a book. She was in her underclothes. She would walk or sit about unclothed in front of anybody. Even in old age she was not ashamed of her body.

"What happened?" Naly asked from the door. "The boiler nearly burst. Who put the coal in after I went upstairs?"

"That swine Utter sneaked in and stoked up the boiler because he wanted me to be killed in the explosion," Valadon replied calmly. Of course, it had been Valadon herself.

Small though she was, she could look formidable. You could not argue with her. She frightened you with her angry, passionate defense of any theory she formulated, however ridiculous or impossible it was.

Valadon also suggested that Utter had cut up several of her paintings because he was jealous of her as an artist. She could say things like this without turning a hair.

She read a great deal, mostly books on painting. Naly would find her in the morning, still in bed, sitting upright, reading a book.

"Italian painting was a lot of rubbish," she announced one morning, waving the book she was reading.

Naly looked at the book: it was a work on the *quattrocento*.

"How can you say that?" he asked.

"They were up to all sorts of tricks. Painting isn't tricks. Painting is what we discover in ourselves."

She was proud of having found her own individual art. She always pursued her own aims; therefore, she had no time for anything that was not straightforward. "There are not only eyes and the brush," she said. "There is the painter too. He is the most important." Harmony was a word she frequently used when discussing painting. She kept Naly up into the small hours, speaking of Lautrec and Degas.

Naly remembers that she burst into his bedroom one morning at first light. She was in her nightdress and in the half-light she looked like an elderly devil. She jumped into his bed.

"Look at this," she cried, opening a book she had brought with her. It was a book on art. "Look at this reproduction. It is disgusting."

"Why disgusting?" Naly asked. She took up hardly any room in the bed.

"That's not talent," she said. "It's just ridiculous. Ridiculous painting always disgusts me."

Having delivered herself of those words she slipped out of Naly's bed and returned to her bedroom. Naly found her still reading when he got up.

Valadon's paintings seldom found buyers and she had no money at all. Now and then Valore came, generously leaving a hundred-franc note on the chimney piece—the new chairman coming to the rescue of the founder of the firm with a sum no bigger than a New Year tip to the coincierge.

The new chairman was not one to spend money on others. When Valore and Utrillo reappeared from La Doulce France and settled in Le Vésinet a dinner was given in their honour at La Bonne Franquette. During the meal Valore left the table and went down the rue des Saules to the Lapin Agile to show her diamond rings to Paulo Gérard. "I invest the money he makes in these," she said, holding her hand up to the light. "I turn canvases into diamonds."

Shortly after they had moved to Le Vésinet Valore called on Valadon. "Maurice is my husband," she said, "and when I say my husband I mean he is now really and truly my husband."

"My poor Maurice," Valadon exclaimed, "so you were impotent all your life waiting for this?"

Jean Metthey decided to have a small exhibition of Valadon's drawings in his gallery in order to help her financially. Naly warned Metthey not to give her more than a hundred francs at one time, for even in her poverty she remained a spendthrift. One day she said to Naly, "We are going to Metthey to collect money." They took a taxi to the gallery. Naly wanted to pay the driver, Valadon insisted on keeping him. "But you'll spend an hour at least with Metthey," Naly objected. Valadon said that to let the taxi go was out of the question. She had come in that taxi and she would return to the Butte in it. She became excited when contradicted, so Naly thought it wiser to keep the cab.

"Going back to the villa?" Naly asked as they emerged from the gallery.

"I must buy face powder first," Valadon said. "I haven't any left of the kind I like. It is between ocher and red in colour, a very special powder, the most expensive I know. You can't find it in Montmartre."

She stopped the taxi in front of every *parfumerie* and chemist's in the Faubourg Saint-Honoré. Naly went in, Valadon remained in the cab. Naly brought out the most expensive face powder he found in the shop and showed it to her.

"It's the right colour," Naly would say.

"How much?"

"Sixty francs."

"No, the one I want is more expensive. Let's move on."

The search for the right powder lasted for two hours. Eventually Naly found a powder at eighty francs. "That's the one," Valadon said when he told her the price. They motored back to the Avenue Junot. A parcel was hanging from the door handle. Valadon unwrapped it to find a box of the same powder brought by a female admirer. Naly went inside with her. A Louis XV writing table stood in the corner of the dining room. "This is where I keep my face powder," Valadon said. She opened a drawer: it was crammed with unopened boxes.

Valadon paid the taxi driver 60 francs, the powder had cost 80, and Metthey had given her 150. The remaining 10 francs were just enough to buy food for the cats.

"It was part of her nature to throw away money she badly needed. It was like wanting to sleep under a bridge," Naly said.

A *charcutier* in the rue de Clignancourt admired Valadon's work. He spoke of it to Naly, from whom he bought water colours, and inquired whether Valadon could be persuaded to paint a small picture for him. Naly spoke to her and she agreed. She painted a red rose in a white glass which Naly found enchanting. So did the butcher. "How much does she want for it?" he asked. Naly went back to consult Valadon.

"*Voilà*," she said. "I want him as long as I live to supply me every day with a quarter roast chicken and half a *langouste*."

"I am sure the *charcutier* will agree to that," said Naly. "Better than cash which you would spend at once."

"But he must deliver them," Valadon said. "Otherwise the deal is off."

The butcher promised to deliver the quarter-chicken and the half-*langouste* every morning. His errand boy came with the first delivery and was tipped handsomely. She even gave him a glass of wine. She enjoyed her cold meal, telling Naly it was wonderful to be able to eat chicken and *langouste* for the rest of her life. The next day the errand boy was again tipped but received no wine. On the third day she ignored him and left the *langouste* and the chicken untouched. On the fourth she hurled the *langouste* and the chicken at the poor boy's head.

"Who do you think I am?" she shouted. "A fool who has nothing better to do than eat chicken and *langouste* for the rest of his life?"

So the butcher acquired a Valadon painting for one chicken and two *langoustes*.

There roamed on the Butte a gentleman known as Tambour. He had no profession and did not work. He spent his time trailing from one bistro to another. But he looked a mysterious sort of person, and Valadon became interested in him, for even in old age and illness she retained her curiosity and interest in people. She asked Tambour into her home. He stole a drawing of hers while she was out of the room and sold it on the Butte. The dealer who bought it recognized Valadon's work and showed it to Utter, who then went to remonstrate with her.

"You can't have a person like that in the villa," Utter said.

"I'll ask him in again," Valadon answered. "I like him. He reminds me of my circus days."

Jean Vertex had an open car and thought Valadon would enjoy being taken for a drive. He asked her and she accepted with pleasure. Vertex expected her to wish to be taken to Vincennes or the Bois de Boulogne or the Parc de Montsouris. She chose, however, to be driven through the narrow, noisy, smelly streets of the Marais, the Faubourg Saint-Antoine, Ménilmontant, Belleville and the lowest purlieus of Vaugirard and Grenelle. She enjoyed the outings most when it rained.

She did not talk during the drives. Her little head was covered with an old shawl which she pulled down over her forehead. Her eyes were alive with curiosity.

During one of the drives Vertex reproached her for painting less and less. "It is better to take one's own measure," Valadon said, "and stop in time. I knew the giants of painting who gave me all they could give and all I could absorb. I learnt from their example. I found myself, I fashioned myself and, I think, I have said all I have to say."

None the less there was still a last exhibition of her paintings in Metthey's Galerie de l'Élysée.

Valadon suffered from uremia and had a heart attack on April 6, 1938. Utter was away in Saint-Bernard, and so Valore took matters in hand. She arranged for an ambulance to take Valadon to a nursing home, where she booked a room for her. But Valadon died in the ambulance at ten o'clock at night as it was passing the Arc de Triomphe on its way to the nursing home. Utrillo immediately had an attack of nerves which prevented him from going to his beloved mother's funeral.

It was a sumptuous funeral in the best Montmartre tradition. Picasso, Max Jacob—back from his country retreat—Rouault and Derain were present. Three speeches were made outside the church of Saint-Pierre, one by Carco, one by André Salmon and the last by Édouard Herriot, who in the course of his funeral oration expressed his dissatisfaction with the government of the day for having reduced the alcoholic content of *pastis* from 65 to 45 proof. When the service and the speeches were over everybody hurried to the Moulin Joyeux for a drink.

Valadon was buried beside her mother in the cemetery of Saint-Ouen. If she, who was born in a small town in 1865, had lived another eighteen months she would have rediscovered in the blackout the dark nights of her childhood. "When you judge me," she used to say, "don't forget that I lived among giants."

Le Vésinet and After

1

W HEN the Germans were advancing on Paris in June 1940, Valore and Utrillo joined the long queue leading out of Paris. The roads were jammed with cars and refugees. Their progress was as slow as that of the others. Many cars were abandoned on the roads for lack of petrol, and theirs suffered the same fate. When the armistice was signed between the Germans and Marshal Pétain, Valore thought it wiser to take Utrillo back to Le Vésinet. He would be safe there.

"When you have such a treasure," she says disarmingly in *Maurice Utrillo, mon mari,* "you have only one desire, namely to keep it in a safe place."

In the autumn of 1947 I came back to the Butte after seven years' absence. Like the rest of Paris it was emerging from the twilight of Occupation. Naly and Utter were the first people I saw. Naly had not changed. Utter had. He looked as though the last seven years had taken twenty years from his span of

life. I asked after Utrillo. They told me that Utrillo and Valore were still living in their suburban home in Le Vésinet.

"What is he like now?" I asked, realizing that Utrillo was
now sixty-four years old. "Much more haggard," Utter said.
"Otherwise there is no change. His paintings are still the same
too."

"Still, there was the escapade," said Naly.

It took place during the Occupation. Carefully guarded,
Utrillo had yet managed to give his wife and warders the slip
and took the road to Paris. They noticed his absence only an
hour after he had vanished. They thought he was in his studio.
By then Utrillo had met a tramp on the road. The *clochard*
in his old suit and with his toes sticking out of his boots was
a familiar apparition from the past. They stopped and smiled
at one another, for fundamentally they had a lot in common.
The tramp took his bottle of red wine from his pocket and
offered Utrillo a swig.

"Where do you come from?" Utrillo asked.

"I come from nowhere. What about you?"

"It is Montmartre for me wherever I go," replied Utrillo,
so the tramp later reported.

When the bottle was finished Utrillo gave the tramp the
little money he had on him, and the tramp went into Le Vésinet,
where he bought wine for the friends to share—not the usual
habit of *clochards*.

Naly and Metthey appeared in Le Vésinet that afternoon.
Valore, who was in a terrible state of anguish, begged them to
join one of the search parties, and it was they who found Utrillo
and the tramp lying asleep in a ditch with the litre of red
wine between them. "It was a moving sight," Naly said. "They
lay there in tender friendship." When they roused him Utrillo
declared he would not return home without the tramp, so they
took him back to the house.

"I am not coming in if my friend isn't invited," Utrillo said,
and for once Valore obeyed him. "He looked imposing when he

said that," Metthey said. The tramp stayed for a week. By then Utrillo had lost interest in him.

Generally, Valore had no more cause for fear. The escapade was the last time Utrillo showed any spirit. (A tramp was not good enough for Valore, nor was the ditch. In her version the man was an honest, toiling road worker and they were found in the worker's hut.) Though he remained a problem for her until the end of his life his resistance amounted only to coarse language, fits of temper and childish petulance. Yet she never relaxed the watch over him. Nobody appreciated better than Valore how much she had to lose if anything happened to Utrillo.

Utter and Yvette had also left Paris at the beginning of German rule. Derain took them to Avignon in his car. Later they went to Saint-Bernard, which Utter sold in 1943. Then they returned to the rue Cortot, and as fuel was hard to come by he broke up some of the old panelling of Rosimond's day in an effort to keep himself warm.

I spent only a week on the Butte in the autumn of 1947. I had a long evening out with Utter. We did the bistros of the Place du Tertre one by one. I did not know at the time that Yvette was no longer living with him, though they still remained friends. In his philandering fashion he was carrying on with a rather attractive woman of fifty before transferring his attention to her less attractive daughter.

Utter, at sixty-one, still drank heavily. His friends would take him home at midnight, wish him a hearty good night, and as soon as the coast was clear Utter would re-emerge and go off drinking again.

It snowed heavily at the end of January 1948. Nights are eerily silent when the Butte is covered with a cloak of snow, and hardly anyone is abroad in the whiteness. Once, after parting from his friends in the rue Cortot, Utter returned to the bistros of the Place du Tertre, where he continued drinking. He was tired and heavy with wine. On leaving the last bistro he sat down on a bench in the deserted square. It was still snowing hard. Utter fell asleep and was almost frozen by the time he was discovered. The doctor diagnosed double pneumonia.

Yvette nursed Utter devotedly. On the eighth day his temperature went down, so all seemed well. The patient felt like celebrating and asked for *langouste* and chicken, a bottle of Bourgueuil and half a bottle of champagne. He was the cheerful, witty André Utter again, and was thoroughly tight by the time he fell asleep. If sleep is the threshold to death, then Utter crossed it quickly. He died in his sleep.

"A fine Montmartre death, truly worthy of him," said his friends.

He, too, was given a splendid funeral and laid beside Valadon and her mother at Saint-Ouen.

Langouste and chicken. It was for this that the *charcutier* bought a Valadon painting. And it was Utter's last meal.

One early afternoon in August of that year I went to Naly's studio in the rue Saint-Vincent. Outside his little red house, one of the last remaining old buildings in the street, stood a long, black car with a burly chauffeur in uniform leaning against it. I went in, and there in the company of Naly and the exotic red fish and deep blue seas he paints was Valore, sparkling with diamonds.

"We meet again at last," she exclaimed as she took my hand. "How marvellous!"

Frankly, I was surprised. We did not know each other well enough to justify such effusiveness. Our meetings before the war had invariably been brief, and when we did meet my attention was focused on her husband. In fact, I should not have been surprised if she had failed to remember me.

"It is so nice to see you," she said, her cruel eyes shining.

I asked after Utrillo.

"The Painter," she said, and you could almost hear the capital P, "is well. But he is so difficult, so very difficult. Isn't that so, Naly?"

Naly agreed that it was so. Then Valore asked me if I had any plans for the afternoon. The one daily recurring pleasure of Paris in August is that you do not need to make any plans. I said I had none, so she asked me to accompany her to a dressmaker's preview of her winter models. Vertex was coming too, and Naly would join us for dinner. Naly signalled that I should accept the invitation. I said I was delighted. Then she spoke of the Ambassador. The Ambassador was tiresome; she could hardly manage to get him away from his *prie-dieu;* yesterday he had even refused to dine; in short the Ambassador was making life difficult. I thought she was speaking of some French ambassador with whom she was well acquainted, yet I was puzzled. Vertex arrived and that gave me the chance to take Naly aside.

"Who is the Ambassador?" I asked.

"Why, Utrillo," said Naly. "She calls him the Ambassador of French Painting."

"Accredited where?" I asked, laughing.

"To Le Vésinet," Naly said dryly.

Valore, Vertex and I drove in her Citroën to Mad' Carpentier, the dressmaker, in the rue Jean-Mermoz. Valore talked all the time and her diamonds flashed in the August sunshine. She seemed bursting with enormous vitality and I could not believe that I was sitting beside a woman of seventy. She was a diligent name-dropper, and anything that came from or had to do with a celebrity was admirable in her eyes.

"You can have no idea how witty Sacha Guitry is," she said. "I was at a reception the other day, a wonderful reception, where *Tout-Paris* was present, every one of us a celebrity. Sacha Guitry came in. He shook hands all round, but when it was my turn he said in a ringing voice, 'I won't salute Mme. Utrillo.' There was general consternation, some ladies looked as though they were ready to faint. What an insult to charming, distinguished Mme. Utrillo. 'What has happened?' cried my hostess in despair. 'We met already on the stairs,' laughed Sacha. There was general relief and laughter." She saw in my expression neither relief nor laughter, so she added for my enlightenment, "That is how great wits amuse themselves."

We arrived at Mad' Carpentier, where she was received as an ambassadress would expect. We sat down on a sofa and watched the New Look. Valore had introduced Vertex as her historiographer. Vertex gave me a wink. Valore grew tired of all attention being focused on the models and in her penetrating voice repeated various dialogues she had had with the famous. Everybody became aware that she was Mme. Utrillo, as, of course, was her intention.

"The Minister said to me, 'Of course, you, Mme. Utrillo . . .' Her Excellency threw herself into my arms, saying, 'How beautiful you look, Mme. Utrillo . . .'" And so on.

In an armchair next to our sofa sat an old lady with a *lorgnon* whom the saleswomen addressed as "Marquise." Valore was interested, but to her annoyance the Marquise did not react to Mme. Utrillo's references to herself. I was chatting with Vertex and looking at the models. When I turned in Valore's direction again I saw that she was talking to the Marquise. The Marquise grunted but Valore was all smiles.

She did not order any dresses, though she had spoken as if she had come to buy the whole shop. When we left she took us to her flat which was across the street. The flat was furnished like any fashionable dressmaker's salon. You thought you were still at Mad' Carpentier, except that the establishment had shrunk. Valore left us alone for a while. Later I found out that she had been down to the concierge, for whenever she had guests it was her habit to acquaint the concierge with their rank and station. When she was alone in the flat and did not feel like rejoining her husband in Le Vésinet, she would spend hours gossiping with the concierge. At heart she remained the provincial girl from Angoulême.

When she came back she spoke again of Utrillo and his *prie-dieu*. "I said to him the other day, 'Are you married to Joan of Arc or to your Lucie?'"

I smiled, but she was quite unaware that the story was against herself. Her next story was even more to the point. Important guests had come to Le Vésinet and she wanted Utrillo to meet them, but nothing could persuade him to interrupt his prayers. "I begged him," she said. "I nearly went on my knees." She clasped her hands as if in prayer. "I said to him, '*Maître*,'" her voice broke, "'my beloved husband-child, Painter, my all, my everything. I beseech you, come and speak to the important guests who are dying to meet you.'"

Utrillo would not budge, she returned sadly to her guests, but then—oh sunshine!—Utrillo appeared. She nearly swooned with joy, opened her arms and cried: "My treasure!"

"You're telling me," answered Utrillo. ("*À qui tu dis.*")

I stared at Valore. How could she tell that story? Was she not aware of what those words implied?

"Neither was Utrillo," said Naly, when I repeated them to him.

When we left the flat Valore said she needed a new hat for the evening. "You must be tired by now of the hat I am wearing." We were driven to Albouy, the most expensive milliner of the decade. Nowhere does a woman give herself away more completely than at a milliner's. She concentrates too hard on her appearance in the looking glass to be able to maintain her poise. I watched Valore in the glass. Her eyes glittered as she tried on one hat after the other. She stared hard at herself. There was no love, only impatience in her eyes. She had, I realized, no tenderness even for herself. Albouy and his saleswomen worked hard. You never saw such an array of hats; and while she surveyed the hats in the glass she harangued the world at large— that is, the whole shop, including the other customers. Her monologue centered round her exalted position as Mme. Utrillo and Lucie Valore. She chatted about the late M. Pauwels, his fortune and his race horses, then about the high opinion Vincent Auriol, the President of the Republic, had of her and Utrillo. But she was not pleased with the hats, none of them suited her.

She shook her head as she said so, and I thought we would leave hatless. However, she pointed to a hat which she had already tried on.

"M. Albouy," she said in ringing tones, "as I am taking these gentlemen out to dinner I want you to lend me this hat for tonight. My chauffeur will bring it back in the morning."

She put on the hat and we motored to the Butte.

She boasted of her painting, for in her own eyes Lucie Valore had become a great painter. She had taken up painting during the Occupation.

"It is hard to believe that a woman with no talent could have cashed in so shamefully on her husband's reputation as a painter," said Michel Georges-Michel, the author of *De Renoir à Picasso, les peintres que j'ai connu,* when we discussed Valore's efforts. "Van Dongen's wife, who was a painter in her own right, gave up painting because her husband was so much better than she."

Valore's attitude was quite different: she took up painting precisely because her husband was a famous painter; and she painted lamentably badly. Utrillo, she told me in the car and repeated later in her book, encouraged her, saying, "Work, work, you have all the potential and the right personality." Even old Tabarant, who should have known better, wrote to Utrillo, "Utrillo! Utrillo! Be proud of Lucie Valore. You have produced an artist of astonishing strength."

Utrillo told both Naly and Metthey that he thought her painting atrocious. But he said it only in a whisper, asking them not to repeat it to her.

Michel Georges-Michel told me an amusing story about Valore's idea of her importance as a painter.

Valore appeared in Deauville at the height of the season. Her first stop was at the shop of the best-known milliner, a woman this time. "I shall be in Deauville for a week," Valore said. "So I need seven hats. You must make me one for each day."

The milliner said that was out of the question as she had too much work on hand.

"If you make me seven hats I will give you two canvases in return."

That impressed the milliner. Two canvases by Utrillo were worth setting aside all other work.

"You will have the seven hats at the end of the week," the milliner promised; and when the seventh day came the seven hats were ready. Valore arrived with the two promised canvases, both wrapped in paper. The milliner kept her impatience under control, and did not unwrap the canvases until after Valore had left with the seven hats. Both paintings were by Valore. Pekingese dogs, badly drawn and badly painted, stared lifelessly back at her from the canvases.

"It is one of the mysteries of Providence," Valore said to me as the car began to mount the rue Lepic, "that I had to marry the Painter to discover my own talent."

Pointing to the Moulin de la Galette, she said, "You know, of course, that Puvis de Chavannes was Maurice's father." I nodded, for it stood to reason that among the putative fathers Valore would choose the only nobleman. "From Puvis," she went on, "he inherited his talent and his aristocratic presence."

"I thought he inherited his talent from his mother," I said.

Valore gave me a dirty look.

In the Place du Tertre we went into Georges' Bar, which no longer exists. Though Valore was enormously gratified by her position in the Tout-Paris she did not neglect her reputation on the Butte. As a matter of fact she attached immense importance to it and was proud of having been elected Empress of Montmartre by the Commune Libre de Montmartre.

While I sat and listened to the Empress of Montmartre, Gazi hurried past the window, his hat pulled down, his cane moving almost faster than his short legs. Since Valadon's death Gazi could be described as the leader of the Extreme Right of the Valadon Party. He had as much enmity against Utter in death as Valore in life. He made no secret that Utrillo had confided in him during a visit to Le Vésinet that marrying Valore was the biggest mistake of his life.

"I wanted to get away from Utter's claws," Utrillo said, "but it couldn't have been worse if I'd stayed with him." To Utrillo, Valadon had become a saint, even if only retrospectively. She had led a pure, practically chaste life; all stories about Lautrec, Boissy, Satie and the others were lies and calumnies invented by Utter, of course. He fought anyone, including Valore and her adherents, who denigrated his *maman's* memory.

Valore was convinced that she could charm her enemies. When she saw Gazi hurrying past the window she jumped up, ran out and called him back. I could not resist joining them. Valore was effusive, gazed lovingly at Gazi and held out both arms while she spoke. Only the tears were missing.

"Gazi, you know how I loved La Grande," she was saying. "She was really a mother to me too. I miss her as you miss her. Only last night Maurice was saying, 'Where is Gazi? Why don't we see Gazi more often?' Come out very soon to Le Vésinet, Gazi."

Gazi was not impressed. "It was like listening to a snake," he said to me the next day. In response to Valore he said he had been to the cemetery of Saint-Ouen that morning to visit his *mémère's* grave.

"I should have gone with you," Valore said. "I hear, Gazi, that a mass was said for her in the church of Saint-Pierre. I was told that the wrong people went to it. We want the right people on such occasions. We have to be careful in such matters."

Gazi lifted his cane to his hat and hurried on.

"A very stodgy person," Valore observed.

From the Butte we went down to Pomme's restaurant and cabaret at the corner of the rue Lepic and the rue Tholozé, facing the Moulin de la Galette. Alas, neither Pomme nor her restaurant exists any more. She died in 1965, two months before Valore. They had only the year of their death in common.

Pomme was an exceptional woman, witty, charming, intelligent and a true friend. She had come to interpreting Bruant's songs by way of the Sorbonne, where she had studied history and geography. She sang them as Bruant intended them to be sung, for she had the right temperament.

When we were ready to go Pomme presented Valore with the bill.

"A bill?" asked Valore, feigning astonishment. "But, my dear Pomme, one doesn't present the Empress of Montmartre with a bill. It is an honour to have her on one's premises."

"My dear Lucie," said Pomme, "if you are the Empress of Montmartre then I am the Pope of Montmartre. You know your history, don't you? Emperors always lost when in conflict with popes."

"I don't follow you," said Valore, trying to show spirit.

"One more reason to pay the bill."

Valore paid.

Utrillo was devoted to Pomme. One day he lunched there with Valore, and Pomme asked him to make a drawing for her. He sent out for paper and pencils and he drew the Moulin de la Galette, keeping Valore waiting, and when she showed signs of impatience he swore at her.

Three days after the dinner Valore called me and invited me to luncheon. What, I still wondered, did she want from me? She found no time to tell me at the meal because she was incensed with Utrillo's behaviour and could speak of nothing else. The day before they had come into Paris for an important function. (Her life seemed to consist of one important function after another.) They were practically at the gates of Paris when Utrillo discovered that the ribbon of the Legion of Honour had not been sewn to the lapel of the new suit he was wearing. He made such a fuss that they had to drive back to Le Vésinet for the ribbon (he petulantly refused to let her find one in Paris), and naturally they were late for the function.

"Mine is a hard life," she sighed theatrically. "People envy me for being his wife, but they don't know all I have to put up with."

Her diamonds belied the sigh.

Valore was not liked. She had her sycophants, but among my friends and acquaintances nobody cared for her. When she wanted to hang two of her paintings in the Museum of Mont-martre, Paulo Gérard objected, saying to her, "You have given nothing to Montmartre, you have only taken." It was generally believed that she married Utrillo only for his fame and the money he earned. That may easily be true yet she gave me the impression that in her hard, overbearing fashion she was devoted to Utrillo, as a hospital nurse is devoted to a difficult patient. "Valore cared only for herself," was the consensus. None the less I still believe the impression she left with me was the right one.

I spoke to her of my admiration for Utrillo's work.

"Come back to Le Vésinet," she said, "but don't praise his early work to him, especially not the white period. That makes him furious. Praise his present work. That will please him."

I found that understandable. When a painter's or writer's early work is praised it is usually to the detriment of his present production. And it is most annoying when there is some truth in it.

In the car she continued complaining. Utrillo prayed in order to spite her. That is at least what her words suggested. He was socially useless. When she took him to the homes of the exalted she always had to tremble.

"And drink?" I could not help asking.

He was drinking, though only watered wine which did him no harm. She had tried to cure him completely, but that did not work. He was now happy with his watered wine. He did not notice the difference.

Was Utrillo, I wondered, not laughing at the world? Could he accept a life of ease and suburban monotony without being aware of how unsuitable it was for him? Was not the watered wine a joke to him?

When I saw him I knew that Utrillo was no longer capable of laughing at the world.

"I don't know whether I can get him out of his studio," Valore said upon our arrival. "You never know with him."

The house in Le Vésinet gave the impression of a quiet, efficiently run, private nursing home with a secret. It would not have surprised me to find police dogs, barbed wire and man traps. Of course, there were no traps, no barbed wire and the dogs were only yapping Pekingese. The wall of the drawing room was covered with a Utrillo fresco, representing, if I remember rightly, the old Maquis. The garden was well kept. The house reminded me of Berthe Weill's words about the flat in the Avenue Mozart. "Life is absent in this house." It was not a place you wanted to tarry in.

Utrillo did make an appearance. I had seen him last in 1939, and the change in nine years was unbelievable. He did not resemble a seedy actor any more. Everything about him was glassy. A white turnip under a *cloche,* I thought. He looked pleased with himself, pleased for a reason he would not let anyone share with him. Now and then he smiled cunningly, as though he alone knew that an infernal machine was hidden in the royal carriage. He sat with crossed legs, fidgeting all the time, and hardly listening except when our respective heights were discussed. He was unshaven and in slippers.

In an artificial voice prompted by the unreal atmosphere of the house I said I admired his work. He had taught me how to look at houses and streets. He had made me understand perspective.

He gave me a glassy look. *"La perspective, c'est enmerdant,"* he said, shaking his head. Then he spoke of a priest who should have looked in on him but had, apparently, forgotten. He elaborated on that for quite a while. "I am going back," he said, interrupting himself; he took my hand in his two hands, then dropped it. He gave Valore a long, malevolent look and left the room for his studio.

She had praised me up to the skies but he had not listened to her. Though she sighed with relief she went after him, and I was left alone for several long minutes.

She drove me back to Paris, where she was spending the night.

"You can see for yourself what life is like with him," she said. "I am of flesh and blood, I enjoy my position, but with him I have always to be on my guard. I was on tenterhooks in case you should say something or one of the dogs do something that would produce a scene. He can't stand the dogs barking. He makes scenes when they bark. How do you expect to live with dogs if you won't let them bark?"

I finally discovered the cause of her interest in me. She wanted me to write a book about her. I said I understood that Vertex was doing so. True. However, he was doing it in French, and she needed one to be written in English. England and America deserved to know the truth. Besides, she had enough material for two different books.

At the time, I was engaged on a life of Charles Edward Stuart, the Young Pretender, a far cry from Utrillo, except for the fact that the Prince also drank like a fish. Still, the trio had fascinated me ever since I came to live on the Butte, and Utrillo was a grand subject for any writer. The same could be said of his mother. I nearly accepted.

"It will be my life," Valore was saying. "You will start with the day I was born and end it with my apotheosis. You will write in detail about my great career on the stage. I can quote the exact words the great Coquelin said to me when I was in my teens but already showed my genius. And my married life with my Belgian husband and all the social success . . ."

"Where does Utrillo come in?" I asked.

Utrillo, she said, did not exist until she came into his life. She saved him from his mother, Utter and the evil influences of the Butte. He was now at the top of his artistic form, painting better than ever. All Tabarant, Carco, Warnod, Dorgelès and the rest had written about him were sheer lies. He had never rolled in the gutter, he did not take to drink until after he was eighteen and all the stories about him were exaggerated. "You saw for yourself how gloriously happy he is." Utrillo only drank because Valadon and Utter were fiends.

I was taken aback by the venom of her tone. "I have too many commitments," I said.

"Think it over. We could make a lot of money with it. Of course, we will collaborate. I will tell you all about it. You will translate me page by page and then I will add my comments and you will translate them back into English."

I told her I would think it over. She rang me the next morning, and I declined, saying I could not fit her book in with my other work. I had made Naly laugh when I reported her suggestion to him. He admitted that it was he who put her up to it. "I wanted you to have a little fun," he said. Valore did not laugh and our relationship lost its warmth. She brought the matter up two years later: I still said no. The battle of the three parties was raging fiercely, as indeed it still is, and if I had wanted to take sides it would certainly not have been hers.

"An unbiased book should be written about them," Alfred Bar said when I repeated Valore's words to him. "Old men forget and the legend kills the truth, especially the legend dished up by Lucie Valore."

Fundamentally, it was Valore who focused my writer's attention on the trio.

2

In *The Times* of May 23, 1966, Mr. Joseph Chapman, for ten years the F.B.I.'s expert on art forgery, claimed that "faking Utrillos is France's fourth-largest export industry." He may well have exaggerated, but the fakes have been there ever since Utrillo took to painting. Already in 1913 Libaude complained that Utrillo signed works which he had not painted himself. Strictly speaking those were not fakes; none the less they added to the huge number of paintings signed by Utrillo that were not executed by him.

When badly in need of drinking money young Utrillo was willing to do anything. Cronies on the Butte, and now and then even comparative strangers, brought their daubs to him, offering a franc or so if he signed them. They knew that they would get more for them if they carried his signature, and Utrillo was ready to oblige if it meant a litre of wine. When he became better known the same colleagues and fresh recruits made fake Utrillos which again he signed for them. Then they discovered that there was no reason to ask him to sign. They could sign just as well as he. Fakes were fabricated on an imposing scale. There was no cause to worry as long as Utrillos did not fetch an exorbitant price. And when the prices rose it was worth taking the risk.

Warnod put the matter in a nutshell as far back as 1928. There had always been plenty of Montmartre painters, but no school of Montmartre existed. The painters had to wait for that until Utrillo unintentionally founded such a school. His pupils were not drawn to the master by a feeling of admiration or affection: it was sheer rapacity. To take Utrillo as your guide meant condemning yourself to painting bad Utrillos. That was no deterrent to those who wanted to profit by his success. Fakes were produced like a popular brand of toothpaste. A lot of young painters earned a few sous with them. Utrillo himself aided them with his way of life, leaving canvases all over the place, in bistros, with rag-and-bone men, butchers, bakers; in short you could pick up Utrillos for a few francs anywhere in Montmartre. The bad paintings he did when in a hurry added to the confusion, for in them you will find hardly a flicker of his genius.

A concierge in the rue des Trois Frères in Montmartre put up young Utrillo for a night when he was drunk and afraid to go home. To repay her for her kindness Utrillo presented her with a small landscape painted on cardboard. She had no idea of its value or of his rising reputation, and kept the landscape for decades. Then in the Bar des Amis, a bistro in her street, she overheard some Place du Tertre painters discussing Utrillo and the colossal prices his canvases fetched. She told them she had one, and when they saw it they sent her to a well-known dealer. The dealer said it was a fake. How could it be a fake? the old woman protested. Utrillo would not have given her a fake. He was not the man to repay her hospitality with a fake. It was easier for him to give his own. The dealer was adamant. He was sorry but the picture was a fake. She tried other dealers with the same result. In the end she sold it to a rag-and-bone man for fifty francs or so. The conclusion I reached when I heard her sad tale was that the painting was not a fake, but a bad Utrillo.

It is not difficult to appreciate why the fakers selected Utrillo. With his sense of perspective and his discovery of the importance of houses and streets he opened up a new vista for them, showing a Montmartre their own eyes would not have seen. And Montmartre landscapes were always easy to sell. "Anybody could paint a bit of sky, a tree and a white wall," wrote Coquiot. He should have added, after Utrillo had shown the way.

Metthey had gone to a suburban dealer to buy a painting. After the deal was clinched, he dined and drank well, and the dealer kindly put him up for the night. He took him to a room, where without looking round Metthey got straight into bed, switched off the light and immediately fell asleep. The sun was shining in the room when he awoke. He thought that he was still dreaming, for the walls were covered with Utrillos. Metthey, Utrillo's own dealer, had not seen so many Utrillos in one place before. Every one was a fake.

Utter's attitude was rather ambiguous. In 1922 a friend called on Paulo Gérard with a Utrillo. At that time Utrillos were already fetching high prices. The friend was broke. He wanted fifteen hundred francs for the painting, but he could not sell it as it was not signed. Paulo took it in order to help out his friend. A few days later Paulo showed the canvas to Utter. "How much did you pay for it?" Utter asked.

"Fifteen hundred francs."

"It isn't worth a sou."

Paulo told his friend that he should take the painting back the moment he could refund the fifteen hundred francs. Next day Utter returned.

"Have you still got that canvas?" he asked. Paulo said yes. "I'll buy it for fifteen hundred," said Utter, and took the canvas away.

Some time later Paulo asked him why he had changed his mind. "I learnt a trick or two when I worked in the quarter master's store during the war," laughed Utter.

Yet he knew a genuine Utrillo from a fake. I dined on the Butte with him and Naly when a local painter showed us a fake he had just finished, saying it was by Utrillo. It looked like one. Utter told him not to be silly. I asked him how he had known at once that it was not by his stepson. "The leaves," he explained. "Maurice's leaves are nervous leaves. Those were placid leaves."

During a law case against a faker who was condemned to five years' imprisonment, M. Gruet accompanied Utrillo to the Palais de Justice to be heard by the examining magistrate. Maître Garçon, Utrillo's lawyer, went with them. The sight of policemen and *gardes républicaines* in the corridors made Utrillo nervous.

"They let you in all right," Utrillo said, "but who guarantees that they will let you out?"

He was not at his best when he was ushered into the magistrate's presence. The magistrate showed him a number of paintings, all of them fakes except for one Utrillo. Because of his prodigious output it had often been said that Utrillo could not tell the difference between a good fake and a real Utrillo.

The magistrate asked him which of them were painted by him. "Only this one," said Utrillo, immediately picking out the one he had painted.

"Why are you so certain that the painting is yours?" the magistrate asked.

"The first time I painted that house," Utrillo replied, "I painted it with twelve windows. That means that from then on I invariably painted it with twelve windows. The faker did not notice that detail."

And that brings one back to the postcards. M. Gruet had seen Utrillo at work when he stayed in Le Vésinet in 1948. He was very conscientious about detail. He feared that if he relied only on his memory he might give a certain house ten or thirteen windows, whereas the postcard showed that it had only twelve.

Fundamentally, the trade hardly needed the fakers. At Le Vésinet Utrillo still painted with the same speed as in the days when he needed a litre of wine. Owing to his lack of practical sense and of interest in other painters, not to mention the isolated life he led, his paintings had achieved harmony, that is, an understanding between himself and his landscapes. The harmony remained though the curiosity that makes an artist progress had deserted him long ago. His mother was driven by curiosity all her life; not so her son. Tabarant found no evolution after 1928, and M. Gruet thinks that the early thirties saw the end of Utrillo's progress. Moreover, the peaceful, organized life at Le Vésinet contained no incentive to experiment. His paintings retained his profound technical knowledge to the last. The painter had aged, not the brush. Any artist is prone to repeat himself; Utrillo, however, outdid them all, and that went for his old age as much as for his youth. Repetition had come long before curiosity deserted him. To paint the rue Norvins fifty times without becoming bored is a sort of achievement. Some were not so well executed as the others, yet the pictorial form was invariably the same.

His mother and the doctors made him paint as occupational

therapy, and in spite of fame and financial success painting remained occupational therapy to the end. "It is a miracle, a constantly recurring miracle," his mother said of his painting. The same had been said of the Douanier Rousseau.

"The more he painted the easier it became," observed M. Gruet. "His ability and technical knowledge were outstanding, but genius disappeared with the years. The pictures he painted during the last decade of his life leave you cold because you no longer feel the warmth of his talent behind the brush."

When M. Pierre-Gaspard Huit, the film director, watched Utrillo painting with cameras and lights focused on him, he could not believe his eyes. Utrillo worked rapidly, hardly ever glancing at his palette, yet without ever hesitating for a second, his brushes moving as if held by some perfectly sure automaton. "It was the most startling experience of my life," M. Huit said, when he told me the story of the film *La vie dramatique de Maurice Utrillo* from its inception to the final bickering with Valore.

M. Huit and M. Weinberg, his producer, wanted to make a documentary on Utrillo's life with a child actor playing the boy Utrillo, a youth acting the young Utrillo, Jean Vinci, the actor, Utrillo the man, and finally Utrillo playing himself as an old man. They approached Valore and she agreed. None the less they put everything in writing because one had to be careful in dealing with Valore, who had strong views about the publicity she thought due to herself.

Before the war there had already been trouble. A serial had appeared in *Paris-Soir* entitled *Roman d'amour d'Utrillo* by R. J. Boulan. It was a partly fictitious, very sensational story about Valore and Utrillo, in which Valore was portrayed as a sort of triumphant goddess of love who saved Utrillo from himself and his mother. It was in such bad taste that a letter of protest appeared in the *Beaux-Arts* of November 18, 1938, signed by, among others, Picasso, Vlaminck, Derain, Creixams and Jean Dufy. The story, the letter pointed out, "is liable to give a false impression of Suzanne Valadon and Maurice Utrillo." The signatories wrote, they said, in defense of the reputation of mother and son. A fortnight later another letter appeared in *Beaux-Arts*, this one signed by Utrillo. He said he found nothing wrong in the serial, thanked the gentlemen for wanting to protect him and his late mother, but averred that he needed no defense or protection, since he had his good Lucie at his side. The gentlemen should leave him in peace, letting him enjoy his happiness in the retreat he had chosen. "Poor slave," was Jean Dufy's comment.

That letter could not have been penned by the same man who wrote to Gay from mental hospitals and prisons.

M. Huit was aware of the difficulty of dealing with Valore yet the film was made with her encouragement, and the last part, in which Utrillo played his aging self, was shot at Le Vésinet. "We thought we were safe," he said.

He found the life at Le Vésinet a blend of the suburban middle class and Utrillo's eccentricity. Fine paintings by Utrillo hung next to eyesores by Valore.

Utrillo was amused and interested in the paraphernalia of shooting a picture. The house was honeycombed with electric cables. Between scenes he went to the kitchen to drink watered wine. The wine was so shamelessly watered that it could not be mistaken even for *vin rosé*. Utrillo drank it with relish. "I'm going to drink my wine," he would proudly say before stalking off to the kitchen.

The mixture was one-third wine, two-thirds water. He drank eight bottles a day of the concoction, proud of still drinking as hard as in his youth. "Wine isn't as good as it was in my young days," he was wont to say. All the doctors who examined him advised Valore to keep up the pretense; and in that she behaved like an intelligent nurse.

She treated him like a child in front of the film people. "Maurice, go and pray," she ordered him. Maurice went to his chapel, dropped on his knees and prayed with the cameras focused on him. "Maurice, paint." Maurice painted the Lapin Agile under the kleig lights. The postcard of the Lapin Agile was in front of him, yet he did not once glance at it. He began to show weariness during the last shots of the film. "He seemed to us like a tired marionette," was M. Huit's opinion.

Dorgelès wrote the script and both Utrillo and Valore read it. In the short film young Utrillo got drunk, had fights, was beaten up, rolled in the gutter, and was taken to the police station. When the film was ready it was shown to Utrillo and Valore. Utrillo was fascinated by his drunken self on the screen. He watched the picture in silence, and made only one remark and that at the end. "It was much worse," he said.

Valore was pleased with the film, but after a fortnight's cogitation and consulting her supporters she decided against it. M. Huit is convinced that she objected because she did not play a sufficiently prominent part in the picture. She wanted to be in it from the first reel onward; but even a film, especially a documentary, could not bring her into Utrillo's life before their marriage. She became a violent opponent of the film, and eventually M. Décave of La Société des Gens de Lettres arbitrated between her and the film company, with the result that four cuts were made. Valore declared that there had been no cuts. That was untrue. At the Cannes Film Festival of 1950 the film won the Prix Lumière.

Valore did not always have her way with her child-husband or husband-child. The child was still as petulant as he had been in the rue du Poteau. Naly lunched in a small restaurant in Le Vésinet with Utrillo, Valore and Valore's fortuneteller. The meal seemed to be going well until suddenly Valore said, "Dear Maurice adores me. Ah, I am his *femme chérie*."

Utrillo started to play with his knife and fork, and appeared to be going to throw them at her. Then he swore at her. "Look, how he adores me," Valore said, and quickly Naly took the knife and fork from him. Valore said no more and Utrillo calmed down.

They walked back to the house, Naly bringing up the rear with Utrillo, and when they reached the railway bridge under which runs the suburban line to Saint-Germain-en-Laye, Utrillo stopped. "I want to see the train go by," he said. The little train arrived, puffing, and when it disappeared under the bridge Utrillo sighed loudly. "Travel," he said. "That's what trains are for. Travel . . ."

Was he thinking of his murdered friend Chaudois and his house at Le Conquet, or the obstreperous mule in Corsica?

"Hurry," Valore called.

"She gave him all the liberty he needed," said a member of the Valore Party to me. "He was no prisoner in Le Vésinet."

Truly, he was given the liberty to paint and the freedom to do whatever his warders approved of. His tantrums were no longer even rebellion. They became insignificant; but Valore showed cleverness in letting him arrange his timetable as it suited him—within reason and within the walls, of course. He could go from studio to kitchen as often as he wanted to drink watered wine. She saw to it that nobody disturbed him while he was working.

He had never cared for comfort. Though the bathroom had hot water, he went to the kitchen on the day of his weekly shave and brought the hot water back to the bathroom in a saucepan. He spilled half of it on the way, his warder-servants wiping up the water behind him. This did not deter Utrillo from repeating the performance a week later.

Valore bought a new car. "I prefer the old taxis of the Marne," said Utrillo.

He did not bother about what became of his paintings after they were sold, that is, after they were taken from his ken. If you gave him news of one of his old paintings or even of the one he had painted a week before he showed indifference.

He rose around eleven-thirty in the morning and lunched at three, usually alone. Valore and her guests had lunched much earlier. After the meal he went to his studio. He did read newspapers but refused to listen to the radio. He alternated between the studio and the garden until nine when he dined. He went straight to bed after dinner. On Sundays he heard mass from the sacristy. "I hate their faces," he said of the other worshipers. He elaborated on that to M. Gruet. "I loathe people," he said. "Nobody ever took any interest in me except my mother and grandmother." In spite of his success and the honours showered on him he looked on himself as an outcast with one foot in a pauper's grave.

One night when M. Gruet dined at the house, Utrillo appeared in the dining room and took his meal with him and Valore. They were served with vermicelli soup, and Utrillo nearly choked as he swallowed a spoonful. He lost his temper and threw the plate against the wall. Then followed the usual scene accompanied by rolling of eyes, grinding of teeth and coarse language.

Yet, in old age I found him almost a quietist. I was in Pomme's restaurant with Jean Dufy. We stood at the bar chatting with Pomme when Valore brought him in. "Look after him, dearest Pomme," she said. "I won't be long, but I have an important function to attend." Valore departed and we took Utrillo to a table and sat down with him. Pomme related local gossip, which she did amusingly. Utrillo laughed at the first story. He laughed also at the second story because he was still thinking of the first. That was at least Pomme's, Dufy's and my impression. He drank an undoctored glass of red wine, then turned the glass upside down to make sure he had drunk the last drop. When he had taken his third glass and asked for more Pomme said, "I don't want to get into trouble because of you." He took it well.

I wondered whether I could not bring him round to speaking of painting and the great past of the Butte. I told him that I had been to an exhibition of Renoir's work.

"He used to live in the Château des Brouillards in the rue Girardin," Utrillo said.

That was all I got out of him.

Others got less. The son of a café keeper of the Butte, who has since become an art dealer, was taken to an exhibition of Valadon's paintings. In the good old days Utrillo had regularly frequented the father's establishment. Now he was brought to the exhibition and dumped by Valore in an armchair. He sat, slumped back, while Valore, of course, did the honours. "He looked completely isolated," said the future art dealer. Utrillo was served with lemonade, and when the young man was introduced as the son of the father whom Utrillo had known well, Utrillo glanced up, his eyes extraordinarily pale, took the young man's hand between his, dropped it, and grunted. A waiter brought a bun on a salver. Utrillo swallowed it in one mouthful, and grunted again.

Utrillo had forgotten that Paulo Gérard wanted to murder him. He came to see Paulo in the Lapin Agile, where he was photographed by the Press then made a bad drawing for the Lapin's guest book. Paulo Gérard went to Le Vésinet to return Utrillo's call. He chose a day when he knew that Valore would not be there. Utrillo was delighted to see him, and spoke of the Lapin in its heyday. He asked after old friends he had known before and during the First World War. "How is so and so?" he inquired.

"Dead," replied Paulo, and Utrillo crossed himself.

The next one was dead too, so were the third, the fourth, the fifth, the sixth and the seventh. "I never saw anyone cross himself so often," said Paulo Gérard.

Jean Metthey and his wife went out to Le Vésinet. Metthey had long ceased to be Utrillo's dealer. The Mettheys also chose a day when Valore was absent. They rang the bell, a maidservant opened the door, and seemed unwilling to let them in, so Metthey pushed her aside and, followed by his wife, went straight to the studio. At one end was the private altar, a statue of St. Joan of Arc and a *prie-dieu*. The room was cut in half by an iron rail. Five Pekingese, barking shrilly, were tethered to the rail. Utrillo burst into tears when he saw his old friend. *"Te voilà,* Jean," he said repeatedly.

"What's that?" Metthey asked, pointing at the rail.

"Dogs," answered Utrillo.

Another visitor to Le Vésinet was Michel Georges-Michel. Valore courted him and often asked him to Le Vésinet because of his position as an art critic.

Utrillo's piano playing was the *pièce de résistance* at every dinner party. "You may sit down and play," Valore would say after they had risen from the table and gone back to the drawing room. Utrillo sat down, smiled ecstatically, looked right and left, waiting for all eyes to be focused on him, then with one finger he tapped out the "Moonlight Sonata."

Georges-Michel saw Utrillo at an exhibition of his and Valadon's paintings. Utrillo had come from Le Vésinet in the company of the parish priest. "Just one more glass," Utrillo pleaded. "If you please. So that I feel strong enough to explain what a prodigious artist my mother was."

Ignoring champagne and fruit juice, Utrillo had a glass of *gros rouge.* He drank slowly, half closing his eyes. "Look, look," he said to Georges-Michel, "my flowers are not a patch on my mother's." Georges-Michel said Valadon's flowers admittedly were different, but why say they were better than his? "She drew better," Utrillo answered, "had more sense of form, more volume."

Long ago Utter had told Georges-Michel that Utrillo was jealous of other people's drinking, and when he took him out he crossed to the opposite side of the pavement if they approached a café. At the time Georges-Michel did not attach any special importance to Utter's remark. Around 1951 he ran into Utrillo and Valore in the hall of the Majestic in Cannes. Valore was drinking champagne, Utrillo had a glass of red wine before him. Valore received Georges-Michel with joyous exclamations, asked him to their table, and immediately suggested that a photograph should be taken of the three celebrities. Utrillo had emptied his glass and asked for more. Valore said he had had enough. Georges-Michel rose to telephone the local newspaper to send a photographer. The telephone was in the bar. After speaking to the editor, who promised to send a photographer at once, Georges-Michel returned to the hall. He found Utrillo in a terrible state, shouting and pointing a trembling finger at him. Valore and two waiters were dragging him toward the lift. "You are no longer my friend, Michel," Utrillo shrieked; and Valore, who a few minutes ago had refused him a glass of wine, promised him a whole bottle if he would only get into the lift. A page went running for the wine. "You are a false friend," Utrillo shouted, "you have betrayed me for forty years. I hate false people." And then the lift door closed on him, Valore and the bottle of wine.

"What did I do?" Georges-Michel asked Valore when she came down.

"Nothing, but he saw you in the bar and thought you were having a drink on your own."

Valore had more trouble with him in the South of France. I was in Naly's studio when she burst in with her tragic tale. "It was awful, you can't believe how ashamed I was," she began, and out came the story, which as usual was more against herself than poor Utrillo. She wanted him to meet some royalty who was in Cannes at the same time. The Prince of Painting should meet another Prince.

"I explained to Maurice how to behave in front of a royal prince," she said. "I gave him lessons in etiquette and protocol. I rehearsed him. I couldn't do more." She put her hand on her heart. "I couldn't! I can say that with a clear conscience. I rehearsed him for the last time only a few minutes before the Prince was announced. I am, of course, accustomed to the company of princes. Maurice stood at my side. 'Now you know by heart what to do,' I whispered to him as the Prince was announced. Enters the Prince, and what does the Painter do?" She lifted her arms. "He drops on his knees and crosses himself."

She looked more surprised than hurt when we burst out laughing.

My friend William de Cazenave, the art critic, was present at a large dinner party given in honour of the famous, aging Utrillo. In the middle of the meal Utrillo rose from the table, went into a corner, dropped on his knees, prayed for a while with his back to the table, then returned to his seat. The dinner continued meanwhile as though nothing extraordinary had happened.

The older he got the more religious he became, and in company, would kiss medals of the Curé of Ars, which he wore on a chain round his neck. He crossed himself whenever St. Joan of Arc was mentioned and after his mother's death he crossed himself when anyone spoke of Valadon. When he travelled by car he stopped in every village to pray in the church.

In 1949 Utrillo painted the scenery for *Louise* at the Opéra-Comique. In 1950 he received the *rosette* of the Legion of Honour, still longing for the lilac ribbon with the academic palms.

On another occasion Utrillo was received with several other painters by Vincent Auriol, the President of the Republic, he backed away from the President who was advancing with outstretched hand, and when there was no more room to retreat he sat down on the sofa which had blocked his backward progress. "This is the first instance in history, dear Utrillo," Vincent Auriol is reputed to have said, "that a citizen is seated while the head of state is standing. Pray, do not rise." Utrillo remained seated.

The Musée National de l'Art Moderne put on a retrospective exhibition of Utrillo's work. Jean Cassou, the director of the museum, thought that the painter should see it. He knew that Utrillo hated crowds, so he arranged that no visitors be admitted during Utrillo's visit. Utrillo arrived accompanied by Valore and M. Gruet. Even the director was not present. Utrillo walked round the gallery without saying a word. Suddenly he went back to a landscape of the white period, stroked it and burst into tears.

"In spite of everything how beautiful it was," he sobbed.

He died of pneumonia in Dax on December 6, 1955. No famous last words are recorded, but a postcard representing the rue Cortot was pinned to his easel in the hotel bedroom. Nine years before, Valore had bought a plot in the old cemetery of Montmartre in the rue Saint-Vincent. Now Utrillo was brought back to his *butt' Montmartre* for good.

"His was a beautiful soul encased in a weak body," said Canon Collin, who had been his confessor at Le Vésinet.

His widow lived another ten years.

3

When I reached this chapter I decided to go to the Butte and ask Gazi to tell me in his own words the miraculous tale of the pebble. It was a Sunday in August, a dull, cloudy day, and though it was only eleven in the morning the Place du Tertre was already crowded with tourists. They milled round the square, seemingly aimless and lost, coming to life only when they stopped in front of the open-air painters, who were industriously turning out views of Montmartre. The views were more real to the tourists than the square and the Sacré-Coeur, for they could take them away and look at them in the safety of their homes at the end of the tour.

Gazi's office is within the precincts of the church of Saint-Pierre. He has the title of Promoter of the Restoration of the Cult of Our Lady of Montmartre. I had not seen Gazi for ten years. I found him unchanged in spite of his having shaved off his moustache and purchased a new, rather natty hat. The cane was the same.

"Tell me the whole story of the pebble, Gazi," I said after

my wife and I had sat down with him at a long trestle table in his office.

"It was not a pebble," said Gazi, "though Suzanne Valadon, my adopted mother, thought first that it was."

About a year before Valadon's death, Gazi, who had moved into the villa in the Avenue Junot, showed her an ikon of the Virgin which he always kept beside his bed. Gazi belonged to the Greek Catholic Church, his position in the Roman Catholic Church of Saint-Pierre notwithstanding. He had been brought up by an aunt who venerated the Mother of God.

"When I grew up," Gazi said, "I steeped myself in Marian theology and raised the flag of the Blessed Virgin for life and eternity."

Valadon, who was anticlerical and, in Gazi's words, an anarchist to boot, called Gazi an idolater and said that religion was nothing but superstition. They had a heated argument which lasted well into the night. Usually Valadon was not willing to give in or see another person's point of view. Yet the next day she said to Gazi, "Our row last night reminded me of the pebble. I forgot it ages ago, but your words brought the incident back. Isn't it curious? I wouldn't have remembered it otherwise."

At the age of fourteen Valadon had still gone out playing with children in the old Maquis. In the course of a game she fell and cut her knee. One of her playmates, a goat girl, took Valadon to her grandmother whose home adjoined the Maquis (now Place Constantin-Pecqueur). The old woman washed the wound and bandaged the knee. Observant Valadon noticed a small object in a glass case. She thought it was a pebble. It was among other family souvenirs. "A pebble?" she asked.

"Not a pebble," the goat girl's grandmother replied. "It is a fragment of the statue of Our Lady of Montmartre." She spoke to young Valadon of her grandfather who had lived through the French Revolution. He had somehow been dragged along by a mob that went to break the statues in the church of Saint-Pierre. He was a religious man at heart, whom fear alone kept in the sacrilegious crowd. After the others had gone he picked up a fragment of the shattered statue of Notre-Dame-de-Montmartre and brought it home. "So you see it's not a pebble," his granddaughter said to Valadon.

"Are you sure?" Gazi asked when Valadon had finished. "Are you absolutely sure? I just can't understand it. So many broken statues were replaced after the Revolution. Why wasn't that one replaced if it ever existed? Nobody on the Butte has ever heard of a statue or the cult of Notre-Dame-de-Montmartre."

Valadon assured him that she was for once not telling an invented story. Now that it had come back to her she remembered every word the goat girl's grandmother had said. Incredulous Gazi, she suggested, should try to find out about the statue and the cult. She got in touch with her old friend Édouard Herriot, who arranged for Gazi to search the Archives Nationales. "But don't speak to anybody about it before you have positive proof," Valadon warned Gazi. The atheist-anarchist had become almost keener than Gazi to discover the truth.

And true enough Gazi found that a statue of Our Lady of Montmartre had been in the church of Saint-Pierre before the Revolution and the cult of Our Lady of Montmartre was even older than that of Our Lady of Paris. When Ignatius of Loyola was in Montmartre he used to meet his companions at 16 rue Cortot. On the Day of Assumption, 1534, escorted by François Xavier, professor at the Collège de Beauvais, he ascended the Hillock of the Martyrs and in the church of Saint-Pierre he dedicated the Society of Jesus to Our Lady of Montmartre. As there was no statue left after the Revolution the cult fell into abeyance.

"It is for you, Gazi, to restore the cult," Valadon said when Gazi gave her the results of his researches. She was so much impressed by the strange coincidence—her argument with Gazi calling to mind what an old woman had said fifty-eight years before—that her whole attitude changed. She saw herself as an agent of the God in whom she had refused to believe. She made her peace with Him and died a believer.

Valadon's death flung Gazi into the depths of despair. He neither painted nor continued his researches but spent his days moping on Valadon's grave.

"Then one day," Gazi said to us, "as I sat on her grave I heard my adopted mother's voice. It was like the crack of a whip. 'Gazi,' she said, 'you are failing in your duty both to the Blessed Virgin and to yourself. Go and restore Our Lady's cult on the Butte.' "

The cult was restored in 1942 in the presence of Cardinal Suhard, Archbishop of Paris.

A new statue was needed. To have a new statue made seemed to Gazi inadequate and akin to an anticlimax. To commission one for money did not appeal to him; it would be merely a commercial undertaking. Then, lo and behold! in a gravel-covered old well at the church of Saint-Pierre a statue of the Virgin was discovered. It had been sculpted in the middle of the last century, and when the church of Saint-Pierre was about to be demolished (it was saved by a committee presided over by the painter Willette), the then priest of the church, who loved the statue, hid it in the dried-up well and covered it in gravel.

"Thus we had our statue," Gazi said. "Think of the miraculous sequence of events that led up to the restoration of the cult."

I thought of old Madeleine, the washerwoman, who for no apparent reason went with her child from the Bastille to Montmartre.

We left Gazi and came out under the overcast sky. There were even more tourists in the square and in the ceaselessly arriving coaches. Suddenly the sun burst out of the clouds, picking out first the walls, then the trees. The Place du Tertre took on Utrillo's colours.

Selected Bibliography

Aegerter, E., and Labracherie, P.: *Au temps de Guillaume Apollinaire;* René Julliard, Paris, 1945.

Alexandre, A.: *Puvis de Chavannes, sa vie et son oeuvre;* Figaro Illustré, Paris, 1899.

Alexandre, A.: *Jean-François Raffaëlli;* H. Floury, Paris, 1909.

Apollinaire, G.: *Les veillées du Lapin Agile;* Edition Française Illustrée, Paris, 1919.

Basler, A.: *Maurice Utrillo;* G. Crès & Cie., Paris, 1929.

Basler, A.: *Suzanne Valadon;* G. Crès & Cie., Paris, 1929.

Beachboard, R.: *La Trinité Maudite;* Amiot-Dumont, Paris, 1952.

Bercy, A. de., Ziwes, A.: *A Montmartre, le soir;* B. Grasset, Paris, 1951.

Boudaille, G.: *Utrillo;* Le Musée Personnel, Paris, 1965.

Carco, F.: *De Montmartre au Quartier Latin;* A. Michel, Paris, 1927.

Carco, F.: *La légende et la vie d'Utrillo;* B. Grasset, Paris, 1928.

Carco, F.: *Montmartre à vingt ans;* A. Michel, Paris, 1938.

Carco, F.: *L'ami des peintres;* Gallimard, Paris, 1953.

Carco, F.: *La Belle Epoque au temps de Bruant;* Gallimard, Paris, 1954.

Carco, F.: *Peintres français nouveaux, Maurice Utrillo;* "Nouvelle Revue Française," Paris, 1921.

Caso, P.: *La vie tragique d'Utrillo;* G. M. Dutilleul, Bruxelles-Paris, 1956.

Cazenave, R. W. de.: *Le Tableau;* "Le Particulier," Paris, 1964.

Champigneulle, B.: *Utrillo;* Editions universitaires, Paris, 1959.

Charmet, R.: *Utrillo Paris;* International Art Book, Lausanne, 1963.

Coquiot, G.: *Maurice, Utrillo, V.;* Delpech, Paris, 1925.

Coughlan, R.: *The Wine of Genius, a Life of Maurice Utrillo;* Harper & Bros., New York, 1951.

Courthion, P.: *Montmartre;* Skira, Geneve-Paris, 1956.

Créange, M.: *A l'ombre de Montmartre;* Vita, Paris, 1933.

Deroyer, M.: *Quelques souvenirs autour de Suzanne Valadon;* "Les oeuvres libres," A. Fayard, Paris, 1947.

Dorgelès, R.: *Montmartre, mon pays;* Lesage, Paris, 1928.

Dorgelès, R.: *Quand j'étais Montmartrois;* A. Michel, Paris, 1936.

Dorgelès, R.: *Bouquet de Bohême;* A. Michel, Paris, 1947.

Douglas, C.: *Artist Quarter;* Faber & Faber, London, 1941.

Fels, F.: *Maurice Utrillo;* F. Sant' Andréa, Librairie de France, Paris, 1930.

Frank, N.: *Montmartre ou les enfants de la folie;* Calmann-Levy, Paris, 1956.

George, W.: *Utrillo;* La Bibliotèque des Arts, Paris-Lausanne, 1961.

Georges-Michel, M.: *De Renoir à Picasso, les peintres que j'ai connu;* A. Fayard, Paris, 1954.

Georges-Michel, M.: *Les grandes époques de la peinture moderne, de Delacroix à nos jours;* Brentano's, New York-Paris, 1944.

Gros, G. J.: *Maurice Utrillo;* G. Crès & Cie., Paris, 1927.

Heuzé, E.: *Maurice Utrillo;* Chanterau, Arcueil, 1954.

Jacometti, N.: *Suzanne Valadon;* P. Cailler, Geneve, 1947.

Jourdain, F.: *Utrillo;* Braun, Paris, 1949.

Mac Orlan, P.: *Montmartre souvenirs;* Chabassol, Bruxelles, 1946.

Mac Orlan, P.: *Utrillo;* Les Editions du Chêne, Paris, 1952.

Mac Orlan, P.: *La chanson des rues;* Carlier, Joinville-le-Pont, 1939.

Mermillon, M.: *Maurice Utrillo;* Braun, Collection "Les Maîtres," Paris, 1948.

Mermillon, M.: *Suzanne Valadon;* Braun, Collection "Les Maîtres," Paris, 1950.

Oberlé, J.: *Utrillo, Montmartre;* F. Hazan, Paris, 1956.

Perruchot, H.: *La vie de Toulouse-Lautrec;* Hachette, Paris, 1958.

Rey, R.: *Utrillo et les peintres de la banlieue;* Exposition Courvevoie, 1960.

Rey, R.: *Quizet;* la Colombe (Levallois-Perret, Seine), Paris, 1944.

Rey, R.: *Suzanne Valadon;* "Nouvelle Revue Française," Paris, 1922.

Salmon, A.: *La jeune peinture française;* A. Messein, Paris, 1912.

Salmon, A.: *L'air de la Butte;* Les Editions de la Nouvelle France, Paris, 1945.

Tabarant, A.: *Utrillo;* Bernheim-Jeune, Paris, 1926.

Valore, L.: *Maurice Utrillo, mon mari;* J. Foret, Paris, 1956.

Vertex, J.: *Le village inspiré;* published by the author, Paris, 1950.

Vollard, A.: *Souvenirs d'un marchand de tableaux;* A. Michel, Paris, 1937.

Warnod, A.: *Les peintres de Montmartre;* La Renaissance du Livre, Paris, 1928.

Warnod, A.: *Ceux de la Butte;* R. Julliard, Paris, 1947.

Warnod, A.: *Fils de Montmartre;* A. Fayard, Paris, 1955.

Weill, B.: *Pan! dans l'Oeil!;* Lipschutz, Paris, 1933.

Yaki, P.: *Montmartre, terre des artistes;* G. Girard, Paris, 1947.

Yaki, P.: *Le Montmartre de nos vingt ans;* J. Tallandier, Paris, 1949.

—— *INDEX*

A Note About the Author

Peter de Polnay was a young settler in Kenya when he was seized with the urge to become a writer. He left for Paris and lived in Montmartre where he soon met Utrillo and Valadon and became good friends with Utrillo's step-father, André Utter. During the war he worked with the French Resistance and was imprisoned by the Vichy Government. But after the War he returned to the Butte and is still very much in touch with the world in which Utrillo moved. Mr. de Polnay is the author of many novels, biographies and travel books.